Life STORIES

MARGARET HAYES

A reluctant missionary

DayOne

First printed 2005

ISBN 1 903087 75-9

9781903087756

All Bible quotations are taken from **the Authorized (King James) Version** unless otherwise noted. This version was in general use in the period when most of the events recorded in this book took place.

British Library Cataloguing in Publication Data available

Published by Day One Publications
Ryelands Road, Leominster, HR6 8NZ
☎ 01568 613 740 FAX 01568 611 473
email—sales@dayone.co.uk
web site—www.dayone.co.uk

Designed by Steve Devane and printed by Gutenberg Press, Malta

CONTENTS

When Margaret asked me to write a foreword for the new edition of *Missing believed killed* in 2001, I closed with this challenge: 'There is so much more that Margaret could tell us. Her long service in the Congo and in Niger has provided her with rich experiences that would be of inestimable value for today's new soldiers of the cross. So, Margaret, we wait impatiently for the sequel!'—here at last is that sequel.

Her story of capture by Simba rebels, posted as missing believed killed, eventual rescue and arrival home to read her obituaries is well known and well told in her first book. But all that was only a small part of the story of this unfaltering missionary who was compared by one national tabloid to Captain Scott and Anne Franks! This is Margaret's personal story of missionary life in the raw. Her brutal honesty, joyful humour, down-to-earth practicality, sincere humility and deep love for her Saviour are all attributes that those who know her well recognize, not only from this story of her long missionary career, but in her everyday active retirement as well.

Margaret's story is a kaleidoscope of divine miracles and sheer hard work, soaring triumph and tragic loss, glorious laughter and bitter tears, spiritual reluctance and fervent courage. Margaret worked at a time and in places far distant from our modern world of mobiles and e-mails, and as a sister midwife she faced traumatic cases that the text books did not mention and that one doctor told me he would never meet in more than sixty years of medicine here in the West. As a missionary nurse in the field of obstetrics, Margaret often had to assume the roles of surgeon, psychiatrist, pharmacist or physician; lines are not easily drawn in the depths of a Congolese jungle or on the edge of the Sahara desert! This is a story that every young Christian should read, to be encouraged that there are still men and women in the mould of Hudson Taylor and Gladys Aylward, and to be challenged to face the true cost of discipleship. We cannot read Margaret's story without laughing and crying, but, more to the point, we will never be proud of our own achievements again. Typically of Margaret she does not mention that in 1987 she was awarded the MBE in the Queen's New Year honours list 'for nursing and welfare service in

Niger'. For her, that was just another of the many surprises in a life full of the unexpected, or, as she herself confesses in closing: 'There is change in nearly every area of life, but God is unchangeable, always the same.'

Brian Edwards
Surbiton, December 2004

Margaret Hayes MBE in 1987

SAHARA
NIGER
Stanleyville
CONGO

CHAPTER 1

Preparing to be a missionary

THE CALL

The call was loud and clear and insistent: 'Go to Congo.' I was in the final meeting of a Whitsun Convention. There had been three speakers—all brothers—and the theme was 'Your walk, your work, your wealth and your will for the glory of God'. The last one, on 'the will', was taken by the UFM (Unevangelized Fields Mission, now UFM WW) General Secretary, Rev. Len Harris, and as I listened I heard this voice in my head, 'Go to Congo.' How ridiculous! I had no intention of going anywhere; my plans had all been made. I had made up my mind to gain three nursing certificates by the time I was twenty-five years old and then to settle down as a ward sister. Nearly all my adult life I had dreamed of this. My nursing training had been very enjoyable; my midwifery training less so, but having the certificate was the aim. I passed all my hospital exams well, and the official national ones too. After some post-graduate experience as a staff-nurse, the longed-for post as a ward sister would be mine. I loved my work and really was very happy in it.

I had been a ward sister for three years when God called me to serve him in Congo (now the Democratic Republic of Congo). To me it didn't make sense. Was I to waste all these happy precious years of nursing to go to Africa? I have a speech impediment: of what use could I be? God was insistent. More training would be required and I had hardly saved any money, for even as now, nurses were not well paid, but God was insistent.

Verses of Scripture were given to me in the course of my daily Bible reading: 'Why are ye so fearful?' (Mark 4:40); 'Who hath made man's mouth?' (Exodus 4:11, when Moses made his speech problem an excuse): 'Being not weak in faith, [Abraham] considered not his own body' (Romans 4:19). The numerous promises found in Joshua chapter one were also powerfully applied. The final promise (which has never failed) was, 'My God shall supply all your need' (Philippians 4:19).

I had decided to spend a day in prayer and fasting, even though I was on duty. It was during that day that I realized I was fighting God and that the fight was unequal. It was with a sense of relief that I submitted to the call of God, but being human, I did say, 'You have promised all these things, please do not let me down.' Of course, he never could or would, but at that stage I had never really had to exercise faith in matters of everyday living. It had been hard living in a non-Christian home. Dad was a lapsed Catholic and Mother a nominal Anglican. I have four brothers and three sisters (all now married) and I am number five, too young for the older four and too old for the younger three. In a way I was the 'in-between'. Living with most of them at the time of my conversion when I was eighteen was difficult, but looking back I can see how God gave daily grace to cope with their mockery. They thought then, and still do now, that I was a religious fanatic.

An appointment was made with the Rev. Len Harris, to meet him at the mission headquarters. Why UFM? No reason I suppose except he had been the main and final speaker at the convention and Congo was one of their fields, but undoubtedly God was in the decision. I told him of my call and of the many reasons why it seemed impossible for me to go. He was very practical and we discussed training. It would entail going to a Bible College, then on to Paris to learn French, then on to Belgium to gain the Certificate in Tropical Medicine. It was agreed that if I could get through all this successfully, we would take it as God's seal upon the call.

The training programme seemed endless. Previously my aim was to finish studies by the time I was twenty-five, but now it looked as though I had only just begun. How much God had to teach me! I went to Bible College. The lessons were hard emotionally and spiritually. None of us likes to have our rough places made smooth, but as God moulded me, yes, remade me, I began to appreciate his holiness and his high standards for my life, in a way always so high as to be unattainable but like Paul, 'we strive' (see Philippians 3:13).

One real lesson I learned there, and one which was to stay with me even to today, was the importance of prayer. On one occasion one of the students was in arrears with her fees, so two of us agreed to meet up after lights out. We crept downstairs armed with flashlights and travel rugs to keep us warm, as the chapel where we were going was cold and draughty. It was there we met with the Lord in intercessory prayer.

The following morning the student in arrears received an anonymous letter, posted *before* we had prayed, containing a cheque for the exact amount of money she needed to pay her fees. When I excitedly told the student with whom I had prayed, she asked why was I surprised—hadn't we prayed in faith, believing?

After this we met on many occasions in the chapel after lights out to pray over various problems and it was exciting to see God give so many answers. It was a lesson which was unforgettable and one which was to carry me through many difficult situations in the far distant future.

OFF TO FRANCE

When Bible college days were over, it was arranged for me to go to Paris to learn French. Miss Gwladys Ashton, a Welsh nurse/midwife and also a candidate for UFM Congo, was also going, and we travelled together.

Before I left for France, my family gathered together for the marriage of my youngest brother. Another brother said I was not to go to Africa, as being the only unmarried one of the family, it would be my duty to care for the parents when they became old. One sister interrupted him to point out that they were parents of us all and no one member was responsible.

Going to France was the first really difficult step to take, as it would be away from the shelter of England. No matter what one's opinions are of our own country, it is always more desirable when living, not holidaying, away from it.

Certainly one appreciates the security it gives. It was interesting to see how France differed from England. I had been there on holiday, but actually to live and work in a country is a different experience entirely.

For the first few days, Gwladys and I went to a French Bible School at Nogent-sur-Marne just outside Paris, where they very kindly found room for a limited number of language students. After the first evening, when we were addressed in English, we were expected to hear and speak only French. This is where sign language comes into its own!

After this, we registered at a language school in Paris and were given our student cards of identity. After four or five days at the Bible College, we were called into the Director's study, and asked if one of us would be willing to go and live with a Christian French family as an *au-pair* girl, though we could still attend lectures at the school. The parents of the Chevallier family needed care during the daytime while their live-in daughter was teaching at a nearby school. I cannot really remember why I decided or was chosen, but in the wisdom of God, he allowed me the privilege of going to live with the Chevallier family. Obviously my language needs were great, and God knew the end from the beginning.

So began the next phase of my training: living with a French family and being unable to speak French. Mlle Estelle Chevallier came and collected me and my luggage. We crossed Paris using the Metro in the rush hour. We both had two large heavy suitcases and travelling on the Metro we had to change somewhere. It seemed miles before we came to the other line (as it does in London sometimes) especially loaded, as we were, with heavy unwieldy cases. My arms felt almost as though they had elongated like gorillas' arms. I did not know enough French to ask how Estelle felt. It was a fairly long walk to the apartment from the Metro, which was on the fourth floor and there was no lift. Somehow we puffed our way upstairs. I had arrived. To say I was nervous puts it mildly—I was petrified!

Monsieur Gaston Chevallier welcomed me warmly. He had lovely blue eyes which danced and a gorgeous goatee beard. Mme Chevallier also welcomed me with the traditional French double-kiss; her sweet and gentle face was a comfort to me. 'Papa' Chevallier (as I later called him) asked if I could cook, and when the answer was in the negative, he asked if I could cook with a book, and I answered as truthfully as I could. 'I cannot cook with an English book, let alone a French one.' Estelle translated all this for me. It was only then that I knew she could speak English. In spite of all, they very graciously received me in their home and family.

Papa Chevallier had a hemiplegia (paralysis of one side of the body, usually caused by a stroke) and Mama Chevallier was almost blind and in chronic cardiac failure. They were a Christian family, and they did all they could to help me learn French. It was a real privilege to have had the opportunity to live with them.

After the first day, Estelle never spoke English with me, though I am sure she must have been frustrated at times with my stupidity. She was a wonderful cook. Very patiently she helped me with my French, though at first she would leave instructions for me in picture form. Obviously she was a real teacher. So if, for example, she drew a carrot then I knew I had to prepare them for her.

One day Papa Chevallier asked me to make an omelette for their lunch. Well I tried but it turned out like scrambled egg. The next few days I tried again, until we had eaten scrambled eggs four days in a row. That fourth evening I asked Estelle to show me what I was doing wrong, and I have never looked back since. However, I also asked her who had taught her to cook, for truly I envied her ability. When she said that Papa had taught her, I must have looked mystified for she then said, 'Didn't you know Papa used to be a chef in a large hotel?' Wow! Not once did he ever complain about my cooking. I must admit though it was a bit unnerving when he asked me to cook a beef steak and he had his watch out to time me: one and a half minutes each side, three minutes in total. So much for French cuisine!

After dinner in the evenings we had a short time of Bible reading and prayer, and Mama would insist that I read the Bible out loud to them. She knew most of the portions by heart and would say it with me, checking pronunciations as we went along.

Estelle gave me books to read, beginning with a child's primer, though before I left I was reading the classics. They would ask me at dinner what I had read and to give a précis of it. It was hard work but it paid off eventually.

While with them, I developed appendicitis and was hospitalized for surgery. That too was an eye-opener on French hospitals to me, an English nurse. A friend from midwifery days was also in Paris and needed work, so Margaret Brown (now Waller) came and took my place, and when I went back, we both stayed on as 'Margaret One' and 'Margaret Two'.

The months with this dear family were months of preparation for the next step, which was to go on to Brussels to continue French studies but with a Belgian emphasis as we were going ultimately to a Belgian colony. From Brussels we went on to Antwerp to study for the coveted Certificate in Tropical Medicine. Surely only God got me through these exams, which were both written and oral in eight different subjects. It was this success which put the seal on my going to Congo.

In the *pension* where we lived in Antwerp there were pictures everywhere, and in my study-bedroom alone there were forty-eight! Those on the staircase began on the ground floor with the subjects being fully clothed and the higher one went, the less they had on until on the third floor they were naked! Another fascinating fact was that there were no fewer than twenty-five umbrellas in the wardrobe of my room.

It had been agreed with the mission that if I could pass the exams in Tropical Medicine—all in French and eight subjects—the mission would accept me, if not I would take it as from the Lord, and I would not proceed any further concerning Congo. The outcome was that I passed, not with distinction, but I passed, and I acknowledged then as now, that only God could have done this. 'With God all things are possible.' (Mark 10:27)

PREPARATION FOR CONGO

I went back to England at the end of March to meet with the General Secretary again. We fixed a date provisionally for August for me to leave for Congo. A week later a call from the mission asked me to go to the mission that same day. Rev. Len Harris asked if I would consider leaving on May 2nd. Just five weeks! By this time I was virtually penniless and we had reckoned on the need of £500 (£500 in 1957 was equivalent to about £7,500 in 2004) for equipment, fare and support. I also needed a team of supporters.

I asked for time to pray about it, and was given one hour. Shutting myself in an empty bedroom in the mission, I asked God to show me how it could be done. Again his promise to supply my every need came back to me, and with such a real assurance combined with the sense of his very presence, I was overawed and could only worship him. The decision was made, papers for signing were taken home, followed by explanations to an incredulous family, and the assurance that every need would be met in the five weeks before my scheduled departure.

A phone call from a family member was to the point. 'Don't think we (the family) will be giving you money. You are on your own and will not receive a penny from any of us.' I answered that actually I had not intended to ask any of them for help, but knew that God would supply.

One of my sisters was living at home at that time. She would come home in the evening and ask what had I bought that day towards my equipment, and I would take her up to my room to see. She, too, was astounded at the way God was providing, though she did not see it as God's hand at all. One day she said, 'You came back from Belgium with no money, yet you have bought more things and clothes in one week than I have bought in a year.' God was meeting the financial need. Little by little, money came from friends and anonymous donors until only £70 remained outstanding of the original £500.

My flight was booked for Thursday May 2nd. On the Monday before, my mother asked how much money was still outstanding, and I told her £70. Her comment was that my time was up and it was now too late to receive more. All I could say was that God had promised and would not fail. That same morning a cheque came in the post for £35, and for Mother unbelief was beginning to give way to belief. On Wednesday May 1st, the day before my flight, yet another cheque came for £35. Thus the entire £500 had been met! Mother was as excited as I was, and as we were talking about it, my sister came down for her breakfast. Mother said to her, 'See what the Lord has done for her.' My sister immediately took up the words 'the Lord' and said, 'Hmm, you'll be getting religious like her next!'

That week there had been no fewer than three air crashes and the headlines were screaming the news. My departure was to be by plane. A phone call from a contemporary from Bible College days came while I was out, and Mother took the call. My friend rang to say she was leaving for Nigeria on Friday—the day after my flight. Mother asked her if she was to fly and her answer was 'Oh no! I'm going the safe way—by sea.' Not very reassuring for Mother.

At last, Thursday May 2nd actually dawned, and the family came early. One sister very thoughtfully came before breakfast as she knew Mother would be upset. Our next-door neighbour was chosen as a neutral observer to take me to the air terminal in London, and the family followed in their own cars. All the way there the neighbour kept asking if I was sure I wanted to go, because if not he would happily turn round and take me back to my broken-hearted mother.

The excitement of leaving, along with the natural tendency to feel the pull of home and the known way of life, leaves one with a feeling of bewilderment and almost a mental vacuum. Tears come, but why? Is it joy or sorrow? One can hardly tell, so mixed up are the emotions. After all, I was leaving for a five-year term. As the final call for the coach was made, friends gathered round to pray, and the last tearful farewells were over. My travelling companion was missing but no doubt she would turn up at the airport. The first irrevocable step had been made. At the airport there were more friends and family. There was little time left. The mission staff prayed with us, goodbyes were said, and after a final wave, I was absorbed by passport and customs officials. There were curious glances from fellow-passengers, who had witnessed me praying with the group. It all became blurred in the numbness combined with excitement and, yes, a degree of apprehension.

I met my travelling companion, Miss Isobel Whitehead as she was then; she was going back to Congo for her fourth term. Her first words after greeting me were: 'Where is your missionary helmet?' It was packed in my equipment, which I hoped was now en route by ship. As I write, I can smile but at the time Isobel kept on about my missing helmet (it was a twenty-four hour flight in those days) and how cross the Field Leader would be when he met me without my helmet. I was not looking forward to meeting this man with my first act of unwitting disobedience to field rules. However, we gave ourselves up to enjoying the long flight. We touched down at Khartoum at 6am and I saw my first glimpse of Africa and an incredibly beautiful sunrise. We re-embarked and excitement was rising.

At 10.30am precisely on Friday May 3rd we touched down at Stanleyville (now Kisangani) airport. God had brought me this far; now I was to see how he would undertake for me in so many marvellous ways.

CONGO AT LAST!

The air conditioning in the plane did not prepare me for the heat wave as I stepped out on to the tarmac of Stanleyville Airport. It was like opening an oven door. Isobel had excitedly pointed out the mission folk, but I did not really identify them until we actually met. They included the much dreaded Field Leader, Rev. Herbert Jenkinson (affectionately known as Kinso even to this day). Whether or not he noticed my lack of a helmet, his kindly eyes did not betray, but I noticed that most of the other ladies did not have one.

Customs clearance was cursory; we belonged to that despised race called 'missionaries'. In many countries missionaries were despised and ridiculed (in some places they still are) by the colonials or expatriates who were in positions of authority, an authority enhanced by the then abysmal illiteracy of the people in whose land they had chosen to live. Happily this era is now passing, but to me it was the beginning of the cultural shock. The missionaries seemed a jolly crowd. Isobel and I were put into cars and the rest climbed into the back of a small truck which had a wire netting covering, rather like a cage, but they did not seem to mind.

It was, of course, impossible to absorb all I could see and hear. It was a bad road, which would deteriorate later on. There were real palm trees, blue skies and hot sunshine. This was Congo at last! It had taken three years from that first day when God called me. We turned into the driveway of the children's home, a large spacious place, cool and dim. I met so many folk; some I supposed had come to see if I would fit in somewhere.

Asani Benedict, later to be the mission's senior pastor but then an evangelist (he was one of identical twins), was there. I had heard much about him and had prayed for him, and here we were face to face. He looked quite ordinary—what did I expect to see?

The hubbub of meeting people, people meeting one another, questions and answers, laughter, teasing, shopping problems; was it only twenty-four hours away from London? All the missionaries looked and sounded human. I was still at the stage where they were very much on a pedestal. Their names I knew; now faces were added to their names.

Mrs Ione McMillan, an American and mother of six healthy boys, and her Canadian husband, Hector McMillan, were in charge of the children's home. Ione put me at ease with her gracious welcome, and showed me my room. The missionaries drove into town to do their shopping. I unpacked, bathed and changed. Being a newcomer to a missionary family is a strange experience. Everybody seems to fit in except oneself. They are self-assured and know when and where to help with chores, know the routine, speak the language and enjoy such good personal relationships that the newcomers feel left out. I suppose it varies with temperament but I found it overwhelming to meet the big names for whom I had long prayed. Were these then the tired, overworked, underpaid (let's be honest) pioneers of our mission? They looked like normal human beings. What had I expected? This was a question I repeatedly asked myself in those early days.

At noon the children who were at school came home for lunch, the school bus putting them off at the driveway. They were noisy, demanding, and gregarious, in short just children. They ranged in age from six to fourteen years, boys and girls. That particular day I ate with the missionaries. Lunch was not extraordinary. The dessert included a fruit I had not eaten before: papaya. I did not like it but ate it, as I did not want to appear finicky, especially at my first meal on Congo soil. Lunch was followed by a siesta and I was grateful to lie down in peace. It had been a tiring twenty-four hours with an enormous emotional output, having left home and friends and arriving into a new situation. I slept heavily.

One of the things which amused me at that time, and on looking back still does, was as follows: it was mid-afternoon on that first day. I had walked outside the house to investigate when I saw three statues of three small boys. They were so very lifelike I walked over to see what kind of sculpturing it was, only to see all three suddenly disappear into the long grass. How foolish I felt when I realized they were three boys who, being surprised on seeing me, had stood stock-still until I made a move towards them. A seasoned missionary explained that one becomes used to being stared at all the time. This was another lesson in my new culture, but one to which I never really became reconciled.

I worked with the McMillans for the first three months, helping to care for the children and was duly dubbed 'Auntie Margaret'. Several things come to mind as I write. I would watch the children in the lounge, sitting in a semicircle, some on chairs, some on the floor, listening to Hector McMillan as he took family prayers, hearing him ask the children questions and the children's ready responses. He did not bypass the difficult Bible themes. I can vividly remember the day we studied Hebrews 12, and he read about a father chastising his son. Suddenly he shot a question at his three year old son Tim, 'Timmy, why does Daddy spank you?' and Tim's ready answer, 'Because you love me, Daddy.'

Another memory is of the day Hector went to siesta with the children, ostensibly to make sure they rested properly while we women cleared away the lunch things. About half an hour later the lounge door slowly opened and in crept all the children on tiptoe, shoes in hand. Quietly the door was closed by the last one. The leader put his finger to his lips and Ione was going to ask what was going on. 'Sh-sh, Uncle Hector is asleep and we don't want to waken him,' he whispered. It took some time for Hector to live that down!

A weekend spent at Wanie-Rukula, a bush station about 40 miles (75 km) outside Stanleyville, comes to mind. Miss Thelma Wild (now Mrs Southard), a Canadian in her third term, took me there soon after I arrived in Congo. In some places, the road was just a mud track recently awash with rain. We slithered and skidded and as the journey progressed my admiration for Thelma's driving ability went up by leaps and bounds. The bridges, just wooden planks placed over tree trunks, made me hold my breath but Thelma didn't seem to worry too much. At Wanie Rukula I met the intrepid and tireless Kerrigans, both pioneers from the mission's early days. They were known as Kerri and Ma Kerri by all and sundry and this too persists to today. Here I saw at first hand a real mission station. The mud huts, the forest almost on the doorstep, the tiny church. Thelma's house I thought delightful and looking back I now wonder why. It was a simple, three-roomed mud hut with simple furniture, no glass in the windows, and a funny little bathroom with half an oil drum cut lengthways for a bath. Hot water was obtained by lighting a fire outside the bathroom under another drum of water.

I now knew a few Swahili words, notably 'mutoto', meaning 'child', and 'jambo', which was a greeting. I can remember the surprise someone had when on greeting him enthusiastically and shaking his hand I said, 'Mutoto Mutoto'. As he was a grown man he had reason to look surprised.

CONGO WORSHIP

My first church service was an eye-opener. We sat for two hours on a rough and backless wooden bench. I remember the enthusiastic if not very musical singing, the grating of a toad's voice (I thought it was a squeaky hinge on the window) and listening to a couple sing a duet. As the lady had a small baby, she breastfed him at the same time. Looking round the congregation, I realized that no one thought this strange. The preacher was Tom Logan, still in his first year as a missionary in fact, and he preached for the first time in Swahili. Thelma told me afterwards that he had made several mistakes, but he had at least one member of the congregation who, though not understanding a word, thought he was very clever!

I was struck by the vivid contrast between my own clothing and that of the Africans. My dresses were all new and in fashion, theirs were rags and some children were naked. Strangely enough on reflection, I only felt pity for them. It was many years later that I began to be ashamed of being so well dressed, that is, by African standards.

My very first medical job was to advise Thelma on how to treat a tropical ulcer. These are painful ulcers, usually on the lower limbs, and if not treated very quickly become deep, large and smelly. My first reaction was to say the patient, a child, ought to see a doctor, but there were no doctors in the vicinity to see and Thelma had to do the best she could with what she had to hand—there were no sterile dressings, and no bandages as we know them. I was to see my first 'sheet bandage' in use. There were no 'normal' bandages available at that time in Congo, so Christian supporters in Europe would cut old sheets into strips, roll them up and send them out to us. There was some antibiotic powder available, which I suggested she should use. I was very disturbed inwardly to think there was no other medical opinion to which to turn. In the light of later days this seems silly now, but then I was only four days away from home and Britain's National Health Service. The contrast was vivid and has stayed with me right up to now.

That evening a little boy came to Thelma's house and told her he wanted to 'turn his heart', the Swahili way of saying he wanted to be a Christian. Though I could not understand a word, it was thrilling to see Thelma talking with him, showing him the Scriptures and praying with him.

Thelma took me to Wanie Rakula several times during those first three months in Stanleyville. I can remember seeing a little boy doing arithmetic. He had to subtract two from five. He used his fingers, but as he turned down his middle finger, the next one turned down too. He then turned down his little finger and of course that left him with only two. He had my sympathy: mathematics is not my strong point either!

One evening at Wanie Rukula, Kerri was late coming back from Stanleyville where he had gone to pick up Joe Wright, our Irish Secretary, who was visiting the field for the first time. We were all in Ma Kerri's house when the two men arrived. Apparently, the car lights had failed and they had driven back by starlight (no street lights in the jungle), and over those awful bridges too—no wonder Joe Wright looked pale! Kerri, of course, shrugged it off with his usual aplomb, as one of those things that happen in Africa. I marvelled that one could really get used to things like that.

During those first three months we had a Family Conference which was held at another station called Banjwade, 40 miles (75 km) away in another direction from Stanleyville. The roads were good compared to the Wanie Rukula road, though it was in fact always referred to as a 'washboard top' road, because of its corrugated surface.

We met for business as well as for spiritual renewing. The ministry was inspiring and the fellowship wonderful. I felt very new. It was good to meet Dr Ian Sharpe and his wife, Audrey, again, both of whom I knew from working in London and studying in Belgium.

It was decided during this conference to send me to a station called Maganga to relieve during someone's furlough (home assignment). Before I could go to Maganga I first had to attend the Government Hospital in Stanleyville for one month in order to be allowed to practise anywhere else in Congo and obtain a work permit.

This was an interesting time; a time of mixed emotions, when I saw things happening which would never have been allowed at home, and which we as observers were powerless to rectify. The wards were administered by nuns, but the rest of the staff were local people. Standards were low, conditions appalling, and the smell of some of the wards nauseating. There were three nurses from our mission and none of us could communicate with the patients unless they spoke French. Very few knew any French, and we were still to learn the local language. My time at the hospital finally came to an end. I repacked my things and was transferred from the children's home to Maganga, just four months after my arrival in Congo.

Life on the mission field

Before I go on further about the work in Congo, it will help to know a little of the background against which we worked. Belgian Congo, as it was then called (now the Democratic Republic of Congo) was a land of marked contrasts: of Cadillacs and the humble hammock slung between two poles, of trained doctors and witchdoctors, of highly skilled professionals and illiterate huntsmen, of beautiful spacious houses and mud huts barely able to remain standing. Wealthy people flaunted their cameras, radios, cars and clothes to the very poor people in the bush who relied on the drums for their news and amusement. They walked barefoot everywhere, their clothes were made of cheap cloths, and up to the age of five the children ran around naked. Shoes were a luxury and food monotonous, hard work to grow and prepare and precious little of it anyway.

The Congolese are like people anywhere; they too have their emotions, their likes and dislikes, their tears and laughter. They also have souls which can be saved or lost, and for which Jesus Christ came. In short, they are people like you and me but with a different background and culture. My work took me into the bush and I worked with four different tribes. Each tribe has its own language and customs, though to me, the new outsider, it took time to recognize the difference.

MAGANGA

Maganga station was about 90 miles (145 km) from the city of Stanleyville, tucked away along a side road called the Kondolole Road. When I went there Mrs Betty Arton and her husband had gone home to the UK for furlough. Betty was a nurse/midwife as well as having the tropical diseases certificate: the latter was necessary to register a dispensary. Mrs Nora Parry had been left alone to carry on the medical work. Nora was from the UK. She too was a nurse, and mother of four young children, two of whom were away at school, and the other two, being preschool, were with her and her husband, Dennis, who was an evangelist. Also on the station was Miss Mabel Wenger from the USA, with such a big heart she had legally adopted three Mulutto children, Louise, Christine and Joe. Jeanette, Louise's child, was also included. These folk formed the nucleus of my new family for the next year.

Maganga had no electricity, no running water (therefore no plumbing), lighting was provided by oil lamps, the refrigerator ran on kerosene, and water was collected from the run-off from the roof when it rained, which was frequently. My bath consisted of a forty-gallon petrol drum sawn in half lengthways and supported on four stones, and a Heath Robinson contraption carried water to the bath from a bucket high up on a stand outside the window. Water was warmed by the sun, necessitating a warm bath before sundown! The hand basin was a bowl on a table; the toilet was outside—a hole in the ground with a little mud hut over it, a home for spiders, scorpions and lizards!

EMERGENCY BIRTH

It was the day after my arrival at Maganga, and I was still unpacking, when Nora Parry called me to say there was a woman in labour, who couldn't deliver, and please would I go and do a forceps delivery? Forceps! My mind boggled at the thought. I told Nora that it was impossible as I had never done one in my life before, and the patient would have to go to the city (90 miles away). Nora laughed and said quite cheerfully, 'We don't send forceps patients to the city, and anyway it is too late. As a midwife of course you can put on forceps.'

With my heart thumping terribly, and praying for all I was worth, I reluctantly followed Nora down the path to the maternity unit, and oh my! The patient was lying on an African type bed, made of bamboo slats, and only 6 inches (15 cm) off the mud floor. Sure enough she needed help, but where were the forceps and were they sterile? Nora said they were in process of being sterilized, and to my incredulous eyes there they were—in a black cook-pot, over a wood fire, the water boiling away merrily and the handles sticking out of the top!

That God was the God of the impossible I truly believed, and the words 'I can do all things through Christ which strengtheneth me' (Philippians 4:13), I really had to believe. I thought of all the white tiles and sterile packs in the hospitals at home, drew a deep breath and scrubbed up. Nora prayed with the patient in Swahili—still an unknown language to me at that time—and I prayed in English. Prayed! It was more a cry of distress and despair! Well, God heard my prayer and to my astonishment and no doubt the patient's relief, God performed a miracle and the baby was safely delivered, the forerunner of many such miracles. Our prayers of thanksgiving afterwards, though in incomprehensible Swahili, had a very heartfelt 'Amen' from me. The baby was a girl with a good pair of lungs, and as she was my very first Congolese baby was named Margarita—again the first of many so named. A very wet-behind-the-ears missionary went thoughtfully back to finish her unpacking.

This all must sound very easy, but it was a very enervating experience and one which made me realize that if God was going to work through my hands, I would have a lot of reading to do to upgrade my professional knowledge. Happily most of the textbooks which I had brought with me were really for doctors.

EATING CATERPILLARS

During this induction period, I had a very charming girl called Louise Bruggerman, the now adopted daughter of Mabel Wenger, to interpret for me and initiate me into some of the cultural mores of our part of Congo. One day, early in my days at Maganga, Louise took me behind the scenes to meet the women in their kitchens. As they worked in the open air it was easy to watch the food being prepared. One lady was busy stirring some bubbling palm oil in a cook-pot over an open fire. I asked Louise, 'What is she cooking?' The answer was 'Caterpillars!' I thought Louise was teasing me, but they were really being deep-fried. The challenge was put to me by this lady. 'Would you like to taste one?' Nothing was further from my thoughts, but Louise wisely told me to say 'Ndio'—Yes—and then to hold out my cupped hands to receive one. It really was a caterpillar! Louise then suggested I eat it. I hedged by asking her to eat one too. She did, showing me how to nip off its head and tail, pop it into my mouth and look as though I enjoyed it. And I actually did enjoy it! Honestly! I was then given a handful to munch upon as we made our way from house to house. Louise added that the women were pleased I had not despised their food. Over the years I was to eat many such caterpillars as well as ants and locusts. Something deep fried in palm oil equates with our fish and chips, I suppose.

Our day began officially at 6.30am with a station prayer-meeting. As it was in Swahili it did not mean much to me, but Dennis Parry who was teaching me Swahili insisted I learn by heart the concluding prayer of blessing. Thereafter, if I was at the prayer meeting I would be called upon to close in prayer. No doubt I made a mess of it, but the Congolese are very patient.

PRIMITIVE CONDITIONS

I would like to mention the reaction I had to the primitive conditions under which I had to work and under which the local people had to live. We had been told about them in Bible College and when meeting with missionaries at home, but even so it is difficult to grasp the full picture with our own cultural background. It is only by living in these circumstances that we begin to understand.

The dispensary was a mud and wattle building. The mud had cracked in several places and looked like a dried river bed. The roof was thatched with banana leaves, and leaked like a sieve, and where the rain came in there were corresponding holes in the mud floor. Spiders, ants and lizards played havoc with the inside, large webs formed almost overnight and lizard droppings were all over the place. Ants were in every conceivable vessel and the woodwork was undermined by the white ants (termites). The furniture in this my first dispensary was rough. Packing cases had been made into tables and chairs. The instruments were antiquated, and in places the nickel plating had worn off. The beds were wooden slats fixed together, standing on four legs: no mattress, no pillows and little in the way of blankets. For me, coming from a London hospital the cultural shock was tremendous and though these conditions were a challenge, I admit I found it very depressing and needed to pray for and claim grace daily before going on duty.

Dispensary began at 7am immediately following the prayer meeting. In the makeshift waiting room we began with a time of prayer and a five-minute gospel message. It was no use having it longer if the people were in pain or had children who were restless and fretful, as concentration was difficult. We first saw patients from the workmen from the compound, then the school children, then the villagers, many of whom would have walked several miles to get there and after treatment would have to walk back in the hot sunshine.

It was while I was at Maganga that the Asian 'flu' pandemic of 1957 reached us. First one, then another went down with it, until the entire station— patients, boarding school children, leprosy patients, missionaries and their families—was affected. The only exceptions were Nora Parry and I. We cheated a little and gave penicillin to everybody. There were no complications and no deaths. God surely heard our prayers for help. It was a week when we rarely saw our beds and we were exhausted. My learning curve was very steep!

Mabel Wenger came from Pennsylvanian farming stock. She kept chickens and ducks and took much pleasure in teaching this Londoner how to care for them, lessons which stood me in good stead in later years. I kept chickens as a hobby all the time I lived in Congo—free range of course!

One amusing incident comes to mind as a result of my diagnosing my young house-servant as having filariasis. This is a disease in which microscopic worms are found in the bloodstream, and when looking at them on a microscope they can be seen wriggling. Wisely or unwisely I let him look down the microscope to prove to him I knew what I was talking about.

Reluctantly he began treatment and a side effect is that the patient feels wretched for several days. He was sitting in his mother's kitchen when he felt something crawling on his tummy. On investigation it was only a caterpillar which had escaped the cook-pot, but the lad was convinced it was a filarial worm which had escaped from his body. He refused all further medication, even though everyone told him it was only a common garden eating caterpillar!

One day Mabel Wenger and I had gone to take a baby clinic. Mabel used to do the evangelizing and interpreting. We travelled in her car, but she had let me drive it there and back. We had arrived on the station, and there were only 200 yards to go. I needed to take a sharp right hand turn, went too wide, hit a payapaya tree which just slowly folded in half. I was so surprised and carried on watching it, that I forgot to straighten the wheel and we went into a mango tree.

We had four heavily pregnant ladies on board as well as four other children, none of whom was hurt. In fact not one lady went into early labour—again only God could have intervened in this situation.

As Mabel put her arm round me and asked if I was all right (her car was out of commission for three months), we were watched by a group of teenage girls who were waiting for Mabel to beat me up. The fact that she did not, but even went further and tried to comfort me, made a big impression on them and as they said, this was 'truly the Christian life in action'. So God was able to use the occasion to reveal the effect that being a Christian has on our lives.

Soon after my arrival at Maganga, I was at the dispensary one morning, just clearing up, when a young woman came to me with some material in her hand. Nora translated for me that the woman would like me to make her a dress in the same style that I was wearing. Apart from what I did at school and in the Girl Guides I had never made a garment on my own, and certainly not without a pattern. Nora was amused to see incredulity and then bewilderment on my face. When I said I didn't know how to make a dress, she laughed and said it wouldn't take long to learn. She told the woman to leave the cloth with me and I would do it for her. When I told Mabel Wenger, she too laughed and made some remark to the effect that it would be the first of many. In the end, I unpicked a dress, created a pattern from it and eventually made the dress. The fact that I did not know the measurements, and that the finished product did not fit, was immaterial—I had made my first dress, and, as Mabel had prophesied, it was the first of many.

LEPROSY PATIENTS

It was also at Maganga that I met my first leprosy patients. At that time the Belgian government kept them segregated, and there was a group who lived at Maganga. In return for treatment, food and lodging, they worked on the compound. In many ways it was a rewarding time, for many were saved. Being on the compound year in and year out they heard and understood the gospel.

I do not think any book or lecture can really prepare the mind for the shock of actually seeing one of these poor sufferers who were advanced in the disease. True, I had seen films and photographs, studied the disease clinically in depth and in the laboratory, but even so, I was not prepared to see men and women with stubs for fingers, no toes, sunken nose-bridges, clad in rags, with shoes made from old car-tyres, and with terrible ulcers on their feet. Because of the disease they had no feeling and were not aware of sores and blisters. I was distressed to see burns on a woman's stumpy hands because she could not feel the heat of the saucepans. I can remember one man saying that a rat had chewed off a toe in the night and asking for some kerosene to bathe his feet as a deterrent to the rats.

It hurt more than anything to see them shuffle in line to receive treatment, and to realize that once upon a time they were normal healthy people. Strangely enough, though they looked so repulsive, I do not think I ever felt repulsed; I just wanted to love them all. I felt ashamed of my new clothes and sandals; the contrast between us was so wide. Happily those days are passed, there is no more segregation, and with new treatments mutilations are seldom seen. Even so, once the case is diagnosed it still means several years of treatment.

Two days a week, Mabel and I went out to the local plantations to hold clinics. Plantations were known by name according to how far they were from the big city, e.g. 'KM 102' was one place we visited regularly. We would hold a pre-natal clinic followed by a baby clinic, and while I did this, either Mabel or a local evangelist would gather together a group of women and children, and would preach the gospel. This was no easy task, for if you can imagine fifty to sixty women with an equal number of small children and sometimes more, the noise they made had to be heard to be believed.

INTERFERENCE IN THE WORK

When a woman was due to have her baby, we would persuade her to come back with us to await the baby at our maternity unit. I am sure many only came for the car ride, but it gave them the opportunity of hearing the gospel on the compound. Usually on these visits we would meet the plantation owner—who would offer us a cold drink, say he did not believe what we taught, but if it made his people happier and healthier he was happy to go along with it.

Then one day it happened! Mabel and I went out as usual and we arrived at 'KM 206', a coffee plantation we visited each month. Nobody was around. Usually at least some children would be curious enough to watch us unload and set up our things. This day nobody came. Mabel, who knew the ways of the Congolese better than I, guessed something had happened, for we walked through the drying sheds and the Africans turned their backs to us, and when Mabel asked what was wrong, they shrugged their shoulders and simply said, 'I don't know.'

We made our way to the planter's house and he was obviously ill at ease with us. All he would say was he didn't have anything to do with missions, and as long as his people were kept healthy he didn't mind which mission took the responsibility. Still baffled, we made our way back to the car and the place where we normally held our clinics. Two women were there and they cleared up the mystery.

The Roman Catholic priest and nuns had been there the day before. The priest had told the people that if they attended their clinic, which they were going to begin then and there, all would be well. If anyone attended our (Protestant) clinic the following day or thereafter, the man of the house would lose his job (and this invariably meant his home too) and if they persisted he would be imprisoned. Sadly, we packed our belongings and left the plantation for the last time. We then called into the two or three villages we always visited on the way home, only to find them deserted except for a few elderly folk who all told the same story. Thus at a stroke our outreach in the Maganga area was closed down.

However, there was one bright spot. About 6 miles (10km) from us, along the Kondolole Road was a plantation, and the mission was on good terms with the planter. We treated his sick and delivered the women's babies. The open door continued, but not without cost to the planter. He was visited and threatened by the local Roman Catholic priest and was told to send his people to Batama Dispensary, a further 18 miles (30km) past us. Obviously this was a ridiculous suggestion and the planter refused, whereupon he was told he would be unable to sell his coffee as the market would be closed to him, but the planter continued to patronize us. As far as we know he did not lose his market, at least not until political disturbances overtook the nation.

An interesting fact emerges after all these years. Those plantations and villages are no more, and Batama Dispensary is no more, but Maganga, though impoverished and decimated in population, is still there and faithfully the gospel is being preached.

AFRICAN ADVENTURES

The cultural background brings unexpected difficulties. For example, we knew that some of the population were only one generation from cannibals, but did not reckon that we would be given that title too. Apparently the canned corned beef we bought had labels which said, 'Mammy's Corned Beef' with a picture of an African woman on it. With their logic they said a tin of peas had a picture of peas on it, a tin of beans a picture of beans on it, and so on. Hence a picture of an African woman on the label meant part of her was in the can. This led to the inevitable conclusion that if we were eating it, we were cannibals. So we had to stop buying that particular brand—a pity, for I like corned beef! About this time we were also accused of eating the head of a recently buried man. Despite all our denials, the grave was re-opened, and then that was the end of that episode.

We had some odd visits from wild animals, and at times elephants would wander on to the compound at night. I had always to take two large saucepan lids with me on night calls, so that if I saw an elephant I could bang them together and scare it off. Chimps and gorillas would occasionally come on to the compound and steal our bananas. We normally bought a whole head of bananas and left them out in the open to finish ripening. This was always a great temptation to the neighbouring primates. Snakes in the house were commonplace and we kept a 'snake-stick' in every room in our houses. I can remember a prayer meeting when we were all praying and a voice called out loud 'Snake!' so we all lifted our legs and feet while continuing to pray. One of the men dealt with the snake.

One day we needed to take a man into the city for an amputation of his gangrenous leg. He had his wife with him and some live chickens, including a large, vocal cockerel. The man's leg smelled badly, so we kept the windows open. Further on, we sprung a radiator leak, necessitating my getting out with an old hat to fill up with water at any river we passed. The cock crowed loudly every time we stopped and on arriving at the hospital proclaimed our arrival, much to everyone's amusement. After we left the hospital we heard an odd noise and found the fan belt had broken. We managed to limp to a garage to have it fixed, and could only praise God it had happened after we had left the man and his cockerel. God's timing is always so perfect.

In Congo we always prayed before making a journey. When everyone was on board, just before the ignition was switched on, someone would pray for journeying mercies. Considering the state of the roads and the complete lack of service stations, the surprising thing was that someone did not pray all the way.

On one occasion, Mabel asked if I would like to go with her on a weekend evangelistic trip. I jumped at the idea, very selfishly thinking that Nora would have to do all the medical work and be on call. I went with Mabel. The car was loaded as though we were moving house. Louise came with us. We stayed at a *gite*, a house put aside for expatriate travellers, sparsely furnished and maintained by the local administration. Much of the weekend is a blur in my memory. We went from village to village holding impromptu services of about an hour's length. I was amazed at how many we did in one day. Mabel was indefatigable. Whether she preached the same message each time I do not know, for Swahili was still a largely unknown tongue to me. I can remember Mabel talking with some people who came to the *gite* to see who we were and what we were doing. Mabel said afterwards that when she asked them how much they knew about Jesus Christ, they wanted to know if he was her husband! They were not being funny: they had never heard of him before.

After about ten months in Congo, I began to have a lot of migraine attacks. I had suffered from them over the years, but now the attacks were more frequent. I would attend clinics usually with a bowl nearby, and aspirin (the only analgesic we had apart from morphia or pethidine) did not help at all. Our doctor from Bongondza station called in one day on his way to the city, and said he would call in on his way back with some tablets. He did so, and the tablets helped to shorten the attacks, but not the frequency. It was therefore arranged that I should transfer to Bongondza after I had taken my first year Swahili exam—which to my surprise, I passed. Mabel said I could have Louise with me at Bongondza. The people there spoke Bangala (a dialect of Lingala) and as Louise spoke Bangala she could help me learn it. After much prayer we packed and a truck came to take us to Bongondza. So began a new phase; one which was to be packed with incidents and experiences.

That God was in the move I had no doubt and subsequent experiences only served to enhance my total dependence on the Lord and his wisdom.

Bongondza: the next phase

I was at Maganga for only a year. During this time, I was busy learning language, customs and culture as well as working hard in my own role as a nurse/midwife. I was also coping with my own housework. As a result, I was not really aware of how much I had learned until I went to Bongondza. Here there was a larger number of missionaries, each with varied ministries. It is therefore a convenient point to summarize all I had learned about the Congolese, and help to set the scene for further activities.

CONGOLESE CUSTOMS

As a rule the Congolese are an hospitable race, always ready to share what little they have. Often I have seen a visitor arrive at mealtimes and always invited to eat. Some customs are universal to all, for example, when food is prepared, the menfolk come in and eat first. When they have finished, the women and children have what is left. If a visitor arrives the amount left over is that much less. To prepare food can take several hours, so it is not a question of opening cans and adding something; the women and children just go without if there is not enough.

If the village is near a river, the dishes and pots and pans are taken and washed on the bank; if not, water has to be carried from the river to the house. Tea towels are not necessary; the dishes are placed on the leaf roof of the house and dried in the sun.

Cooking is done over an open fire, each family having its own. In the evenings the smoke rises slowly over the village, giving a sense of oneness. It is always a source of amazement to me that more children are not burned or scalded, for at an early age—about three years—they are taught to blow the embers into flames and how to arrange and rearrange the logs. Sometimes the family has two fires, but more often than not only one, which means only one item can be cooked at a time, so cooking is kept to a minimum, usually once a day, and that in the evenings. Mornings, the cold leftovers, if any, are placed in a banana leaf and reheated in the embers of the fire. Wood for fires is carried by the women and children, usually from their 'gardens', which would probably be a mile or two away. As a rule, it is the man's job to fell the trees, but the women chop them up for firewood.

Each village owns land surrounding the village and the boundaries are clearly defined—to African eyes. It is on this land that each family is allotted a 'garden', which is about the size of a large field. The land is measured out per family in January (the dry season). The menfolk go along and fell the trees, and considering this is part of the large forest, this is no mean feat. One can only admire the courage of the African in preparing the garden. Trees are felled, leaves and undergrowth burned, then the ground is cleared and prepared for sowing. By this time it is February, and the husband has made a little shack on the edge of the clearing and then the women and children move in. They work together as a family, cutting, burning, planting and cooking. Even the tiny children are occupied in preparing the food or scaring off the birds which come looking for the seeds. Only the sick or elderly remain in the village. A young woman due to have her baby will still have to go; maybe she will have her baby one day and be hard at work the next. The dry season lasts three months and there is much to be done if there is to be food and firewood for the following twelve months. The gardens are cultivated in rotation, so that each family may have two or three in use from previous years, depending on the crops.

When the new shoots start to show, the men return to the village, leaving the women and children to fend off the birds, then by this time the old women go to the garden and help with them. Children return to the village in the evenings with food for the men, sleep there overnight and return next morning.

The day starts at dawn, about 6am, and there is little respite all day. Most go to bed after the evening meal. With only oil lamps, the light is poor. Also oil is expensive, therefore it is cheaper to go to bed.

The food can be monotonous, plantains (a cooking banana), rice or manioc being the staple diet, supplemented with a dish called pondu or sombe made from manioc leaves cooked rather like spinach, then finished off with palm oil and chillies. It takes time to acquire a taste for this and get used to the chillies, but once acquired is usually very popular—I could and did eat it every day. Peanuts play an important part in the diet and are either boiled, roasted or pounded into peanut butter; they are rich in protein. Meat is frequently chicken, goat, wild boar or elephant. Usually it is hard to get meat in the bush and expensive in the cities, so the men go hunting with spears, bows and arrows and knives, using nets to ensnare an animal. In season there may be antelope, monkey, porcupine and forest rats, as well as caterpillars and ants. Sometimes a family will go a couple of weeks without meat. A tin of sardines or pilchards is a luxury. Bread, too, is a luxury and few in the bush have it. Fruit is usually abundant, being mainly citrus fruit, pineapple, star fruit, bread-fruit, banana and avocado. Tomatoes are usually very small, bitter in taste and need lots of camouflage in cooking.

Nearly every family has chickens, kept mainly for eating. The eggs are allowed to hatch, though, as frequently happens, an epidemic of fowl pest can destroy hens for miles around. The ones which survive are small and scrawny, as they do not have food supplements and have to manage as best they can, truly free range birds.

Church services as a rule follow the nonconformist pattern, with a decided African bias. Even so the services are still long, with lots of items on the programme. The congregation participates more than we do in the UK, and the singing, if not always tuneful in our terms, is always joyous.

The church buildings are simple. Nearly all bush or village churches are mud walled and leaf-roofed, with very uncomfortable logs on which to sit, or else none at all, and the congregation bring their own chairs. At least it takes away any formality.

Services are announced by drums, usually one hour, fifteen minutes, then five minutes before the service begins. The drums play a large part in village life; they call to church, to school, announce births and deaths, arrivals and departures. With no telephones (and years before e-mails), they are lifelines with the outside world, as well as acting as clocks. Not everyone had radios, and batteries are difficult to obtain. The 'wind-up' radio is a recent invention.

There are many customs which to us may seem trivial, but to the Congolese they are a part of everyday life. Receiving something with both hands cupped together may look greedy and rude, but it is the polite way, and the two hands together mean 'Thank you', so it is not even necessary to say the words. At first I was surprised by such 'bad' manners until it was explained to me. Afterwards, I always did it, and once or twice found myself doing it at home in the UK—much to my own embarrassment!

A gift, no matter how small, is always given with the right hand, as this apparently includes a blessing. Using the left hand implies an insult. Truly these are small things, but can be enough to reverse weeks of patient teaching. Placing money in the offering or taking communion is always done with the right hand.

Often in visitation, the visitor is invited to share the meal, and this again needs much tact. If one really has not eaten, it is simple enough to accept, though I was always ill at ease in so doing, for I knew they had so little. If I had eaten and could honestly say this, then the thing to do was to retire gracefully, for it is the height of bad manners to watch someone eat!

A custom which took me a long time to figure out was the one appertaining to twins. The parents would reverse them, twin one becoming twin two and vice versa, and throughout their lives this order would be maintained. The switch is done in a belief that it would confuse the evil spirits. Our pastor twins were a case in point. Pastor Bo was first-born and Pastor Asani the second, but it was always Asani who was the leader and to whom deference was paid. They were, of course, born to unbelieving parents.

Another odd custom relating to twins is not to name them until they themselves 'decide' their own name, so for eighteen months they are known as 'One' or 'Two'. As soon as they begin to talk, the grandmother—who had chosen their names at birth—begins to teach them to say 'my name is Paul' or whatever name is chosen, then when they can say this, they are taken to their parents and announce their names. During this nameless period the mother is not allowed to cut, wash or comb her hair, cut her nails or bathe. Also she must only wear navy blue clothes. It is therefore brings great relief all round when children can say their names. Of course, Christians do not follow these customs.

To have twins means hard work; there are no cots or prams. The babies sleep with their mother on her bed, and in the daytime one is carried behind and one in front. Of course, the one in front gets all the nourishment. Often in baby clinics I would find one twin thin and very underweight, and the other fat and overweight. If the thin one died it was considered no great loss. Gradually this attitude is beginning to change, and both twins get a fair deal.

ON TO BONGONDZA

We travelled west and crossed on the ferry. This was like a huge raft with outboard motors attached and ramps at both ends. We drove on and on westward on the main highway, a washboard road with muddy patches and very large potholes as well. These potholes were really big, enough sometimes to accept a car, but they were obvious as they were filled with water. On the dry sections of the road we stirred up clouds of red dust which settled slowly on us. Finally, we made a right turn into an uncared-for narrow road, with tree trunk bridges, muddy ditches and a sprinkling of crashed cars. Eventually we reached our destination.

MEDICAL EXPERIENCES

Bongondza was a medical station with a hospital and also a large primary school catering for grades 1 to 5. There were more houses, this time cement block ones with tin roofs and glass in the windows, but these were the missionary houses. The group consisted of eleven adults, seven singles and two married couples, together with five children.

Again there was no electricity, and although we had running water, it came from a large tank which was fed by the excessive rainfall. In North East Congo the rainy season lasted nine months, followed by a relatively dry 'dry-season'. The humidity was high and the average temperature all year round was between 26°C (80°F) and 32°C (90°F). We were very near the equator, and dawn was around 6am. For six months of the year it became dark by 6.15pm with rapid twilight, and the other six months it came at 6.30pm-6.45pm.

On my first day on duty at the hospital, I met Janet Cowger, an American nurse/midwife, and Valerie Buckingham, an English nurse/midwife, Dr Norman Streight and his nurse wife, Nora, both from Canada. There were many African staff and they kept out of my way most of the time.

OPERATING CONDITIONS

Many memories come flooding back as I write—for example, learning to do skin grafts. After the doctor had given the patient a spinal anaesthetic, he would leave me to get on with it. This was fascinating but tedious work. At another time, a patient was brought in semi-conscious. He had fallen, hitting his head. We had no X-ray or scanning apparatus, but Norman thought the man had a blood clot, as he became and was becoming more deeply unconscious. Where was the clot? That was the question. As his condition deteriorated, Norman thought he ought to operate, but he was not a neurosurgeon; neither did he have the proper instruments for cutting through skull bone. Norman took a brace and bit from his carpenter's kit, boiled it, and meantime we prepared the patient for surgery. Anaesthetic was unnecessary as the patient was comatose by this time. Of course, we prayed beforehand and could only leave it with the Lord. Norman drilled a small hole on one side, but there was no sign of a clot. He drilled another hole: again no clot. A third hole on the opposite side and there was the clot! As Norman removed the clot very slowly, to our amazement the patient suddenly became conscious and complained of a fly walking on his head! A very relieved doctor gave praise and thanks to God. The patient made an uneventful recovery.

Another patient named Bisa was admitted with a very infected knee. Bisa was a chief in his village with eight wives. He was also a very objectionable patient, to such an extent that we ladies were not allowed to go near him. He became very ill, because he kept removing the bandage and applying 'native' medicine to his wound, with the result that the wound became grossly infected. We thought he would die from sepsis. Norman sat with him one night, and all through the night he told him about Jesus. By morning Bisa had repented and asked Christ to take over his life. What a transformation! He was no longer difficult, but co-operative and hungry to know more about Christ. He asked for a Bible; he could not read, but he wanted one. When he went home, his Bible under his arm, he set his house in order and then testified to the entire village about his conversion and how Christ was now his Master and Lord.

About a year later Bisa was re-admitted with a strangulated hernia and needed surgery. He insisted on having his head on his Bible during the operation. He died whilst it was in progress, and the crowd who had watched the operation from outside the window began to sing hymns instead of the traditional wailing. His funeral was spectacular with VIPs attending, and the gospel was preached to hundreds that day.

MOMOTI

That particular tribal group always cooked every ingredient they ate apart from fruit. We had some lettuce available, and I had to explain to my house servant, a lad named Momoti, aged about sixteen or seventeen, that we did not cook lettuce and that I would like some for my evening meal. This information reached his village and aroused interest in some ladies from the church. Momoti asked if I would mind if these ladies could watch me. I agreed, and at the appropriate time, five ladies were arranged in a row in front of my table, and as I ate the lettuce, they uttered cries of wonder and disbelief—much to my amusement. They spread the word, and one day when I said I was going home for my dinner, the hospital staff asked if I was going to eat my leaves!

I first met Momoti in the hospital where he had been treated for many months for tuberculosis, and now he was cured was working as hospital 'tailor' to earn money to pay for his final year in primary school. He started coming to my house for two hours a day, and then when he finished school he would come full-time. While a patient he had become a believer and he tried hard to live accordingly. He had a very bad stutter and was ridiculed at school, not only by his schoolmates but by his teacher too. Consequently he failed his final year—and disappeared. I really needed him, as my work load was becoming heavier.

After four days he came back and came to me at the house. 'I suppose you don't want me now I have failed my exams?' he stuttered. My heart went out to him. So I asked if he was truly a Christian. When he answered very firmly, 'Yes, I am', then I said that I too had a speech problem, as he knew, and what I really needed was someone I could trust, as I would be out of the house most of every day and he would be alone in it. I was more interested in his Christian character than any diploma he might have. Did he think he could do that for me? He became the most loyal and honest house servant I had ever had, and when with me he never stuttered after that!

He would prepare my midday meal and the arrangement was that if I was not home by 12.30pm he was to leave the food in the oven (we had a wood stove) and go home. One day I did not get home until 2pm and there was Momoti asleep in the kitchen with his head on the table! When I asked why he had not gone home he said, 'You are late because you are caring for the people of my country and are too tired to look after yourself. I will wait on you first, then I'll go home.' Dear Momoti! I wonder if he is still alive; he would be an old man by now.

Momoti stayed with me until the day I left, and we worked as a team. I do not think I ever had to ask him twice to do anything. If I was delayed at the maternity unit over a meal period, he would turn up with tea or coffee and some sandwiches for me and, despite all protestations from staff or patients, would insist on my eating and drinking before he left for the house. I had never asked for that kind of service. Truly God had sent me someone who was one in a million.

One day the loaf of bread I had made went all gooey in the middle, so I cut the loaf in half, pulled out the middle, and wrote a note saying, 'Oh Momoti, sopo na ngai azali na mpasé' ('Oh Momoti, I have stomach-ache!'). I put the note in the hole, placed the two halves together and left the bread for Momoti to find. With eyes big like saucers, he showed me the note the 'bread' had written! I later discovered that there was a virus in the house which attacked the yeast. The problem was solved by adding vinegar to the dough.

TRAVELLING ADVENTURES

One day a week I needed to hold a prenatal clinic in Kole, a small administrative post about 15 miles (25 km) away. These clinics were always hectic. We would begin with a short gospel service, followed by a prenatal clinic and then an infant welfare clinic. I can well remember how God undertook for us in a very special way on three Fridays in a row. On the first Friday, Alf Walby, an English missionary who was head of the station, was driving a Chevrolet truck containing helpers, some mothers and babies and me. The road was fairly good and we were able to go without stopping, when suddenly we rounded a bend and went rushing down a hill, only to find the tree-trunk bridge had fallen into the river. Alf slammed on the brakes and the next thing we knew was that we had soared over the river and landed on all four wheels on the other side, but facing in the opposite direction!

On the following Friday, Dick Siggs, an American missionary, was the driver and he had a brand-new Chevrolet station wagon. It had rained earlier in the day and the pot-holes were full of muddy water. Swerving to avoid one, Dick went too far on the muddy road and we landed at forty-five degrees in mud up to the axles. It took two days to get the car dug out. We did not make it to that clinic.

On the third Friday, we were in a Volkswagen van with Alf again as driver. We turned a bend and saw a fully loaded cotton truck hurtling down the hill towards us. As these trucks were notorious for having poor brakes, I thought we were sure to collide and I sent up an arrow-prayer. Alf saw a small clearing in the forest and turned into it as the truck flew past, just catching the end of our van, and hurtled on without stopping. We surely praised God for yet another of his deliverances. This impressed upon me the need to commit every journey to God.

The Walbys had four children, and one morning when they were all at home (some went to boarding school) Wilfred, who was about five, came to me and told me they had had a lovely family worship time, and then asked if I had family worship? When I said 'No' he then asked if I was a Christian, and then asked if I was, why I didn't have family worship. So I asked him who would come to it. He replied, 'Well there's you and…' There was a long pause, then 'Oh Auntie Margaret, you don't have anyone!' He went rushing away to his home to ask his parents if they could adopt Auntie Margaret so that she could attend their family worship. Dear Wilfred, his heart was in the right place!

MORE MEDICAL ADVENTURES

Through a philanthropic society the government allowed the mission to build a maternity block, comprising two wards, office and delivery block, and three houses for 'ladies-in-waiting' plus the numerous kitchens they would need. It was built on the extreme periphery of the mission land and the government said that if we did not staff it they would put in their own personnel. So I was appointed to head up the department. All the equipment was new and of good quality: beds, cribs, linen, lamps, delivery necessities, and office equipment. They had thought of everything—such luxury for me!

We dedicated the buildings and moved in—but one big problem I had was the culture. Patients were not used to bedclothes as we know them, would cover them completely with their own cloths and lie on top. The cribs were used as lockers and filled with all their personal paraphernalia. Their reasoning was, 'Babies don't lie on beds on their own, they sleep with their mothers!' In vain I remonstrated, but had to bow to the culture. We had devotions with patients and staff every morning and evening, though the results were seemingly poor, but again the culture predominated. Women were not expected to make decisions without their husbands' authority. However, it also meant that we had a warm reception in the villages, when both husbands and wives were very open to the gospel.

On one occasion we had a run of five premature babies. Keeping them warm was no problem in the high humidity and temperatures, but feeding them was, so I would go to the ward allocated to them every two or three hours, day and night. One day I went a little earlier than usual and to my horrified gaze, there were all the women, each with her three- or four-pound baby lying on her lap, each one having an enema. In this part of Congo at that time everyone, young or old, had an enema every day—another cultural practice. They used bamboo stems and mini calabashes. How those babies survived I do not know, but it was, I believe, more by prayer than maternal care.

Another time the doctor came to do a ward round, and we took with us the blood pressure apparatus. The doctor insisted on carrying it. When we got to the door the doctor opened it and held it for me to enter ahead of him. When he finally left and I was alone with the patients, I was really told off. In their culture, a man always goes ahead of a woman and the woman carries everything. I was in disgrace. I had a steep learning curve at Bongondza!

Returning home from maternity involved a five to ten minute walk along a very narrow pathway between the trees. One evening I was going home in the dark with a lamp in one hand and patient notes in the other, when suddenly a man jumped out in front of me yelling, 'Don't move Mademoiselle—there's a black mamba (a deadly snake) ahead of you!' With the light from my lamp he was able to see it and kill it, and then when satisfied it was dead said, 'You can go on now.' Almost an African Sir Walter Raleigh! I did not know the man and never saw him again. Surely God was instrumental in that episode.

Snakes were very prevalent in that part of Congo and frequently we would find them in the house, perhaps under a pillow, and I once found three down inside the bed. We needed our snake sticks in every room. It was said that a cat would keep them away, but it is not true. I had two cats and snakes still came. How we were not bitten, I can only attribute to God's care.

One night I was wakened by screams and cries from the hospital. Donning my housecoat and slippers I went over to find out what was wrong. Actually I thought someone had died, such was the noise. In the wards everyone was awake and the only word they would say to me was 'Chui'. I did not know the meaning until someone said in French that a leopard had entered the ward and while sniffing at a lady asleep on the floor had wakened her, hence the screams which apparently scared the beast and it ran out. My problem was how to get back home knowing a leopard was on the prowl. I think the four-minute mile had nothing on me!

When the ladies came to prenatal clinic, we took the opportunity to teach them to sew and make a jacket and bonnet for the baby. At the same time we had a gospel message, and also gave them verses of scripture to learn by heart. If they could recite five without mistake they had a small prize, such as toilet soap or a mirror, and they really tried hard to earn them. I remember asking one lady who had learned her five, if she knew what they meant, and she did. Then I asked her if she would like to become a Christian and her answer really hurt: 'When I have had the baby then I will ask my husband for permission.' A lot of women had their babies at home. Some mothers would die or the baby would die, and this was often due to the awful lack of hygiene of the traditional midwives.

We were expecting a visit from our field leader Kinso and a VIP from London. They were late arriving, so we all went to bed. About midnight I was wakened by loud knocking on my door and was told that Kinso had arrived with the VIP, who was no less than Rev. Alan Redpath. Apparently they went straight to the house of Alf and Eileen Walby, and after the initial greeting, Alan Redpath asked Alf for the latest test match scores—amazingly Alf knew!

I was asked to vacate my bedroom and house, as a single bed was required for the missionary driver. So grabbing clothes, and hastily making my bed with clean sheets, I moved in with another missionary who lived opposite. One amusing episode arose from this. My cat would catch lizards and often bring one in as a present for me, usually alive. I would automatically pick up the poor lizard, throw it out of the window, often followed by the cat. But the unscheduled visitor occupying my bed was not amused by a cat landing on him as he slept and proceeding to play with a lizard. My cat and I were not popular!

CUCUMBERS AND CORNED BEEF

We missionaries mostly had our own hobbies. Mine was keeping chickens. One missionary loved gardening and grew vegetables, using seeds from South Africa. The tropical climate and the surrounding forest ensured that the ground was very lush and she always had marvellous results. Cucumbers were her particular joy that year, and she planted about twelve separate plants.

It happened that the annual field conference was to be held just as they were ready for picking, and I was elected to stay back and man the hospital and keep an eye on the various homes. I was also told that I could help myself to cucumbers. To the Africans these were strange vegetables, and as we ate them without cooking, they were never stolen. The conference was to last ten days, including travelling time. On the first day, I did the round of the houses and arrived at the cucumber patch. To my astonishment, there were cucumbers everywhere. I picked a bucketful and put them in the missionary's fridge, but still the plants kept on growing. Each day I would fill a bucket with cucumbers and take it to another house to put in the fridge. At the end of the ten days every house had cucumbers almost filling each fridge and still the plants grew. I was ever so glad to see the folk return! Other missionaries who stayed the night with us on their way to more distant places also went away with cucumbers. That was the end of the experiment.

Even though living on a mission compound, we were not exempt from petty thieves. We had made a trip into the city for supplies, and I, like the others, had bought items to last for two or three months, including meat, which went into the deep freeze. One evening, shortly after the trip, I went out to eat with another missionary on the compound. On my return, I noticed the bedroom window was open (we always closed windows when leaving the house) and at first I did not miss anything, but in the kitchen the door to the deep freeze was ajar and, you guessed it, it was completely devoid of all meat. Maybe the Lord was preparing me for the days ahead, but all I knew was that I ate corned beef, cold, casseroled or even fried for the next three months. Momoti never complained, but just accepted it; probably in his home they rarely had meat. There was an amusing sequel, but that will come later.

DISRUPTION

Just before the annual conference, word was given that Nora Parry of Maganga was due home on leave, and a nurse would be needed to replace her. We were three singles—all nurses—and one would have to go to relieve for a year. None of us wanted to go—certainly I did not, and as I had already had one move that term, I felt it was unlikely I would be chosen.

How true it is that God's ways are not the same as ours. The other two nurses reasoned that I knew Maganga and had learned Swahili, but I argued against it. Then on the Sunday before the folk went to the conference, God really got through to me: would I be willing to go? No, I was not willing, but during my quiet time that morning there was no peace of heart. I reasoned with God that the maternity unit was very busy; I had put down roots in Bongondza, and what about Momoti? So I decided I would fast and pray all day, and it was about 4pm before I capitulated—claiming the many promises given me throughout the day, and finally I said to the Lord, 'All right I will go if they cannot find anyone else.' There was another medical station at a place called Ekoko, and they had several nurses. Then God told me to go and tell someone. I knew if I did, it would be accepted. So I deliberated in my mind for the rest of the day and all that night. In the morning I knew I had to tell Alf Walby, our station leader, so I went to him quite early, confessed my reluctance to go, and how God had brought me to the place of submission to his will. Alf knew how I felt about Maganga, and to my surprise was visibly moved by my offer to go back there. He said that when the subject came up at the council meeting, he would not say anything unless they came to an impasse. So with my inner peace restored but with leaden feet, I went on duty.

The conference went ahead as planned and I did not go. I heard the cars arrive back after the conference and excited voices, but at that precise time I was occupied feeding a very premature baby in my house. Valerie Buckingham came to see me, and her opening words were, 'Guess who was chosen to go to Maganga?' and I answered 'I was?' She was delighted that she did not have to go and that apparently I had accepted the fact that I had been chosen. Hot on her heels came the Maganga nurse whom I had relieved three years before. 'We're leaving tomorrow morning; get your things ready to go,' she said. There was no way that I would have done this. It was only February and Nora was not due to leave until July 18th. I said I would go there on July 17th. We argued, but common sense prevailed, and it was agreed I would go there in July, and not before.

So what happened? This was 1960, the time of independence for many African countries. Then it was announced that Congo would become an independent state on June 30th, and it duly happened. Ugly rumours went around about plantation owners and what would happen to them; we were disturbed, but prayed much for our fledgling democracy. In the meantime I was winding up my work in the maternity unit, slowly packing all my goods and chattels, coping with a very sad Momoti, who was not only sad at losing his job but also fearful for the future of his country.

I cannot remember on which day of the week July 17th came, but the Sunday preceding I had had my farewell at church, and, between packing, was helping on the general side of the hospital. There had been two major operations and several minor ones, and all of the patients needed some extra care. Then on July 16th a car pulled into the compound and out got Kinso, our Field Director. His words were terse and to the point: 'Everyone is to leave Congo by orders of the various embassies, so I give you twenty-four hours to get ready and leave tomorrow, July 17th!' We were all in shock, local people as well as missionaries. At least I had no packing to do, it was all done, but several of us had pets. With tears I put my cat to sleep and burnt his body. Viola Walker had a large dog, and between us we put him to sleep too. I paid off Momoti, and also gave him some of my household goods I knew he could use in the village, and we both wept.

The morning came. The cars were ready and we just drove away—how it hurt! It was on the journey when I realized that this was the day (July 17th) I was due to go to Maganga! It was an 'Abraham' experience for me—apparently God wanted to see if I was obedient enough to do something he wanted me to do. In a way I was sorry not to go, as by this time I was used to the culture and was more confident, too, in my professional expertise and ability to work in such a culture, but then God's ways are not our ways.

The journey was relatively uneventful considering the heightened tension in the country. Passing one village we had stones thrown at us, but we reached Stanleyville airport in daylight, to find it a seething mass of expatriates trying to meet up with embassy staff or preparing to board a plane which was waiting there. We comprised three British subjects, Valerie Buckingham, Alf Walby and I. Alf's wife and four children had left the week before. We boarded the plane.

We arrived in Leopoldville (now Kinshasa) and it looked chaotic. United Nations blue berets were everywhere, and several planes were on the tarmac, both military and civilian. People were milling about, not knowing where to go or to whom to turn. We were in the same category. We went into a hangar and put our suitcases together. I was told to sit on them while my other two companions went to look for help. One prays in situations like this; they are mainly arrow or SOS prayers, but pray we did. Valerie came back quite quickly having found an RAF officer who was flying out an empty military plane within the next hour, and he would take us as far as Ghana. We boarded by climbing a perpendicular ladder, and finally with hand and foot holds. We were pulled into the plane by an airman, then had a further climb to the next floor and a seat. This was an enormous plane and we were the only three passengers.

In Ghana we were met by a consular official, taken to the consulate and given a bed for the night. Next morning, we rushed back to the airport to board an RAF Comet en route for the UK. The Congolese Prime Minister, Patrice Lumumba, was also on board.

BACK IN BRITAIN

When we arrived at Heathrow Airport, we called our homes and in course of time were duly collected. Most of my family were at home (this all happened before half had emigrated to New Zealand) and when there was time for food, I was told Mother had made corned beef sandwiches as she knew how much I liked corned beef. My face betrayed me, for one sister whispered 'Don't you like corned beef?' I quickly told her about the meat theft, and that I had eaten nothing but corned beef for the past three months! She kept quiet about it.

The time spent at home, though earlier than expected, proved to be God's timing for me. It was great once again to meet the many friends I had made, and visit various members of the family, some of whom had young children. Some were beginning to plan to emigrate to New Zealand.

Before I had gone to Africa, I had a special circle of friends and we would meet as a group two or three times a week for prayer and fellowship. There were a couple of nurses involved. Coming back from Africa I found the group had closed the gap made when I went away. Although I was welcomed back, they had moved on—or was it that I had moved on? It meant I was no longer necessary to the group and as one member said, 'You see, your priorities are different now; you are not on the same wavelength any more.' It hurt, and I had to take it to the Lord and ask for his help in understanding what it meant. I have discovered that it is all part of the cost of missionary service, and I have been able to help other first-term missionaries by showing them what to expect when they go home on their first furlough. Most were unbelieving, but when they met me years later, confirmed I had been right. Priorities had changed, and adjusting to such a different culture had remoulded our thinking.

The time at home meant I could go to a Migraine Clinic to be assessed for treatment, but they wanted an exorbitant sum to cover the cost of three weeks inpatient treatment, and could not understand why I did not ask the mission to pay. They advised me against returning to Congo. I was devastated. I remember walking up and down Harley Street, weeping, and asking God to help me. At the time, there was only one answer—to resign from the mission, which I duly did. They left their acceptance of my resignation open-ended, in the hope that my migraine attacks would lessen.

Several months later, when I was working in a London hospital, I received a phone call from the Clinic. They were experimenting with a new treatment and asked if I would take part. The result was beyond my expectations; soon I was able to reapply to the mission and was accepted. God, who is sovereign, had it all planned out for me and the interlude at home had been his preparation for the days that lay ahead. It was not too long before word came from the new Field Leader, Al Larson. Would I be willing to go to Bopepe village and begin to develop a medical ministry there? The folk had been asking for someone to go there for that purpose for a long time.

Bopepe (pronounced BO-PEP-AY) was a small village half-way between Bongondza and Banjwade and only one other missionary lived there, Mary Baker, an American and ten years older than I. It would mean living with her, and I hardly knew her. My brief was to begin a medical work. But where and how did one begin such a work? Was God really asking me to do that? I felt so unequal to the task. I had many questions, such as: What about equipment? Well, what about it? God had supplied in the past; could he, would he, supply again? I doubted my own skills, but God led me to Philippians 4:13, 'I can do all things through Christ which strengtheneth me' also verse 19, 'My God shall supply all your need.' So, taking God on trust, I wrote to Al Larson and said I would accept the challenge.

I had a few months of preparation and deputation work. I had to buy things to take back, as I had been told all my things left behind at Bongondza had been stolen. In this period, many new prayer partners were made and many promises of help poured in. It was an exciting time, though the nearer the date for leaving loomed, the more I doubted my ability to cope alone. I clung on to God's promises and would plead with him not to let me go in my own strength. If he would not be with me, I could not go it alone!

On arrival in Congo, it was good to meet up with colleagues both new and old. Apparently Mary Baker was in the States having major surgery, so her arrival was delayed, which meant staying in the interim at Banjwade, which was about 35 miles (60 km) from Stanleyville, which had by now been renamed Kisangani. Before independence, it had taken just over an hour to get there, but in the intervening two years the road had not been maintained. It now took two or three hours to get to Banjwade on a very poor road surface, and the forest had begun to take over.

For the next few weeks I shared a small house with a first-termer Irish nurse, Betty O'Neill. We shopped and prepared for our future ministries. It was a special time for praying together and sharing experiences, until eventually we went our separate ways. Betty went to develop primary health care in the region, a heavy and exciting job, and I went to Bopepe village.

CHAPTER 4

Bopepe

I had visited Bopepe several times, mainly in transit to and from Stanleyville, and always had great admiration for Mary Baker who had lived there alone, that is, with no other missionary colleagues. Mary was from Richmond, Virginia, USA, a plump, jolly, middle-aged extrovert. Certainly, never in my wildest dreams had I ever thought of working with Mary, much less living with her, too.

In one way, it was like arriving in Congo for the first time, but there was one big difference. I knew where I was going and what it would be like. The rosy glamorous pictures were no longer there, and reality had already kicked in. It would mean hard work, long hours, making do, losing contact with friends at home (remember there were no telephones or e-mails) and settling in to a different culture.

VERY IMPORTANT VISITORS

While waiting to get to Bopepe, I had been informed that the Director General from USA, Rev. Ralph Odman and another VIP, Dr Henry Brandt, were to visit the field and Bopepe was on the itinerary. Two days before they were due to arrive there, I moved in. I borrowed six of everything, plates, cups and cutlery. My equipment had not arrived and as I had not lived there before, I had no idea what was in the house. In any case, Mary was still in the USA and all her things were packed away.

Bathing would be a problem. The men, five in all counting the field leaders, would need a bath after their journey, and all Mary had was an oval zinc bath such as our mothers had before bathrooms were the norm. Apparently the bathroom floor sloped a little and there was a small round hole in the wall through which the water was supposed to go. Well, it didn't! One man (Dr Brandt) had his bath and I was called urgently to bring a broom. There I left him, trousers rolled up as though he was paddling, which he was, desperately trying to brush the water out through the hole. By this time I felt sure I would be sent home in disgrace on the next plane, but worse was still to come. We had restored the bathroom to order and heated another bucket of water on an open fire outside, and then the next visitor had his bath, only to have the same problem. I handed him the now sopping wet broom and, feeling a little hysterical, began to giggle. He was not amused and asked why I was laughing. My answer did little to settle his ruffled spirits. When Kinso had his bath, he had the wisdom to throw the water out of the window!

That evening we were to eat at Pastor Bo Martin's house, and he sent folk over to borrow the 'six of everything'. As I knew breakfast was to be at 6am it was with trepidation I saw the things go, but Bo promised faithfully he would return them when the meal was over. He meant it, I am sure, but as the programme was a long one, he forgot. So did everyone else except me.

As I was occupied with the men, making sure they had drinking water to clean their teeth and that they went to the correct houses to sleep, it was 11.30pm before it dawned on me that my 'six of everything' had not been returned. I made my way back to Bo's house expecting everybody to be in bed, but the sight that met my eyes was amusing in retrospect, but not at the time. The notorious driver-ants (flesh-eating biting ants) had invaded the kitchen and were everywhere! Yenga, Bo's wife, and the children were trying to smoke them out. Across the room, piled in an enormous basket, were my 'six of everything,' plus others used by about twenty-five people, all mixed up, and unwashed. Dancing up and down to evade the bites of the ants, I finally rescued my 'six of everything.' This had taken me twenty minutes and I was well and truly bitten. Wearily I trudged back to the house, in order to wash up the things. We had eaten a meal cooked in palm-oil and all the things were coated with this thick yellow oil. 'In every thing give thanks' (1 Thessalonians 5:18). I could have cried, I was so weary, but was able to give thanks for the kerosene stove, which quickly heated the water, and for water, which amazingly was still in the house. Finally, with everything done and table set for breakfast, I lay on my bed fully dressed at 2am with the alarm set for 5am. The breakfast went off without a hitch except the VIP was delayed by an hour—an hour I could have spent in bed, I thought ruefully. To be honest it was with relief I waved them off on their next leg of their journey, and wondered if life in Bopepe would always be like this.

LIFE IN THE VILLAGE

When they had gone, I felt I had time to look at Bopepe village. The actual village was populated by committed Christians. In fact, all the adults were baptized believers. They lived in mud built houses with leaf roofs. There were only three houses with permanent roofs, the homes of the two pastors and of Mary Baker. This house was to become my home for the next two years.

In the centre of the village was a large brick-built church with a permanent roof, and tree trunks laid out in rows to form the seating area. The windows did not have glass or shutters and the doorways lacked doors.

Our house was built on a hillock, which was also the home of numerous tarantula spiders. We did have cement floors, and shutters at the windows but no glass, and one side of the house had a wide verandah, which shaded the living room and kept it cool.

We did not have running water, and we paid women and girls every day to collect water from the nearest river, which was some distance into the jungle area. We had a wood stove, a kerosene-run fridge-freezer and a small two-burner kerosene stove we kept for emergencies. Mary had installed a small generator, so we had electricity from 6.30pm to 10pm, provided we had enough diesel oil to run it.

After several days had passed, Miss Viola Walker, a Canadian and veteran of the pioneer days, came to stay until Mary was able to return. I had the benefit of her wise counsel, always so gracious and loving; she showed me at first hand how to begin a new work. How gracious of God to have put it into the mind of the Council to send Viola to teach me!

The dispensary began in the house; we made a little room off the living room into the dispensary. The first day we had ten patients, the next day twenty, and the following day, forty. By the end of the first week it was evident we would need a separate place to work. The patients sat in the living room, on the verandah and on the grass outside. It was all we could do to find a place to eat in private without several pairs of brown eyes following every morsel we ate.

The first baby born was that of the chief's wife. We delivered her in the spare room, although thinking back, I realize that it must have been Viola's bedroom, for we did not have a spare room. In all this Viola was very patient, though she did put her foot down at eating with patients still in the house, and I could hardly blame her.

We prayed earnestly about the situation and the villagers worked on an empty broken down church building, putting fresh leaves on the roof and redaubing the walls with mud. It was not much by Western standards; mud walls, mud floors, holes in the roof where the rain leaked in, but to us it was our very first dispensary at Bopepe. It was divided into three parts, a waiting room in the middle, dispensary at one end, and maternity at the other. The fact that the walls did not reach the roof was nothing to worry about, and nobody had secrets anyway! We moved in on February 25th, 1963.

The waiting room could seat seventy-five and was frequently packed full, and each day began with a Bible reading and about ten to fifteen minutes preaching. A captive audience? Sure, but how else could we hold their attention? We had the joy over many months of seeing lives transformed by the power of the Spirit.

This is a suitable point to give a further insight into Bopepe life. Pastors Bo and Asani (the twins) were the joint heads of the tribal family, but they stepped down in order to do Christian work and the local chief became the titular head. In African terminology, one tribe equalled one family. As foreigners we were accepted into the family—a tremendous honour—and Mary and I had to go along with the tribal customs. Some were advantageous; others less so. Once we bought a sack of rice and left it on the verandah. After two or three days the eldest brother (and village elder) came to ask why we had not obeyed the tribal rule, for as the village elder he should receive one tenth of the rice. We apologized for our ignorance and hastened to comply with the rule. It worked the other way too. When a wild animal was killed it was divided into sections, and according to one's status in the tribe, one received accordingly. Our status was high, on a par with the twins, and we often received a whole leg of a wild boar or antelope. Of course, if the person who had killed the animal was of a lower status, perhaps he only kept the tail, though I am sure they found a way round that problem.

The twins maintained a high moral and strict behavioural pattern in the village. The criteria for residence in Bopepe were recognized by the local church, and anyone who was not up to standard was sent to live in 'little Bopepe', which was literally across the road, until they had amended their ways. They would then be received back into fellowship.

The hunter of 'little Bopepe', when out one day, met a wild boar and was not quick enough to kill it. Instead it gored his thigh from groin to knee. He was carried in on a crude stretcher accompanied by the entire village, wailing. The twins' mother, old Mama Rebecca (not a Christian), made the most noise and fuss and I had to insist on her being taken outside the building. Even then the racket she made encouraged the others and they all joined in. This is a routine tribal custom when there is an accident. Having looked at the long wound and decided that treatment was within my range of skills, I said I could not sew him up if there was any more noise. Gradually the noise abated until one could almost hear the proverbial pin drop. Then I began the job of cleaning and sewing the long wound. He was a Stoic! I put in 32 stitches and there was not a peep from him. Next day, I saw him on the roof of his house repairing it. From that day onwards, whenever I had a difficult case, word would go round that 'Mademoiselle likes to work in silence.' This was a big advantage which I had over my other colleagues.

GOD'S MIRACULOUS POWER

Many people ask if I believe in miracles. Of course I do! So does every missionary nurse and doctor. Because we are nurses does not mean miracles cannot happen. God is pleased to use our hands and minds for his glory. A nurse's knowledge is not exhaustive and usually she has specialized in only one field. Even then there are gaps which only a doctor can fill. To work on the mission field does not give automatic knowledge of everything. One is only too aware of how little one does know. It is truly a humbling experience to see a waiting room with maybe up to a hundred patients, all ill, and know they have no one else to turn to for help. Sometimes I could hardly bear to look into their patient, pain-filled eyes knowing how little I knew. It keeps missionary nurses on their knees a long time, and they are certainly sending prayers to God throughout the day.

Each session was preceded by a gospel message and prayer. Many criticize this as taking advantage of a captive audience, yet those same people don't criticize when we teach mothers child-care before a baby clinic. We have medical knowledge to pass on to enable them to care for their children, why then is it so wrong to pass on spiritual knowledge to enable them to prepare for eternity? The two go together. The services are only ten to fifteen minutes long, but if there is no service they will sit there until their turn to go in for treatment comes along, so they may as well listen to something worthwhile as to listen to village chitchat. They have everything to gain, and certainly everything to lose.

I have digressed from miracles. Only a miracle could have saved the lives of many of my patients, so let us start with Timothy, who was a healthy young man in his late teens. He went with a male relative to prepare his garden (an area about the size of a football pitch). It was approximately 10 miles (15 km) deep into the forest. He had only been there a few days when he cut his finger, and this became infected as a result of neglect. The infection travelled through his body and 'native' medicines did not help. The original wound closed but Timothy became very, very ill. His relative became alarmed and started for home to call for help, but on the way he became ill and called into another garden for help. Someone there was going near his village and would take a message. He caught a lift in a truck, and then it broke down. By this time Timothy had been ill for a week, and was barely able to drag himself about.

The truck was repaired. It started on its way and was soon en route for the big city and all thoughts of Timothy were forgotten. Only when it reached the city did they remember him, but by this time they thought news must have got through, but it had not. Another week went by and Timothy was very weak. The truck came back and the fellow got off to enquire how Timothy was, only to find they still had not heard. Hastily a search party set out and found Timothy critically ill in the hut in the garden. They tried to care for him there, but he was too ill. Word was sent back to his village to send a team of men with a hammock and a mattress. They took it in turns to carry him to Bopepe, taking two days. Every step jarred his body and he fainted several times on the way.

Thus it was that I met Timothy late one night. I had been delivering a baby and it was 11.30pm and my bed was calling me. Mama Ruta, my assistant, whispered that there was a bad case outside, so uttering a quick prayer for help and wisdom I stepped outside to see this crowd of people sitting in silence around a man lying on a mattress in full moonlight. Even by this light it was obvious Timothy was a very sick man. His temperature was 41°C (105°F), and he was in considerable pain. Everywhere I touched him there seemed to be a large fluctuating swelling. There was little I could do until morning as our lamps were not all that reliable. I gave him an injection of morphia and, left on his mattress, he was carried into the little house we used as a ward. Many of his relatives stayed, the rest went home.

Early next morning we took stock of the situation. It was obvious Timothy had something I had never seen in these days of antibiotics, namely pyaemia. This is a form of septicaemia in which pus-forming organisms multiply in the bloodstream and set up abscesses anywhere in the body. In Timothy's case they were large and deep seated.

What were we to do? We explained the gravity of the case to both Timothy and his family. We then explained I was only a nurse, but we could and would ask God for the wisdom in dealing with the illness. This we did then and there. He was too ill to take to hospital and anyway he refused to go. We had no radio contact at that time.

We decided to do our morning's work as usual and then spend the afternoon working on Timothy. Actually I was stalling for time—time to pray, and time to think over the actual treatment. It took two days to open each abscess and we drained away 12 pints (8 litres) of pus, not counting that which ran into the bed or spurted up in the air. One I opened was under such pressure that it spurted up all over my face. I was glad I wore glasses! It took two hours each day to dress his wounds and clean up his bed. He was paralysed from the neck down.

On the seventh day he called me and showed me he could move one finger and one toe. Once the swellings went down we instituted passive physiotherapy. Excitement grew. He was by this time severely anaemic, his haemoglobin being only eighteen per cent of normal. There was nowhere to put a needle. So we started him on iron tablets to supplement the antibiotics, and we prayed, both with him and his family. Mary and I also prayed together in the house.

After three weeks he was beginning to take an active part in his physiotherapy. After four weeks was able to feed himself. Ultimately it took fourteen weeks of much prayer and patient nursing to get him on his feet again. During all this time he heard the gospel daily, and after two weeks committed his life to the Lord and so did his family, who so patiently cared for him. Do I believe in miracles? Who else could have cured Timothy both physically and spiritually if it was not God?

After several months, I was called to the front of the house one day, and there was Timothy. He had walked 3 miles (5 km) on crutches to see me, and when I appeared he just stood there, dropped his crutches and held his arms out, a big grin across his face! We hugged—a very un-African thing to do—but everyone understood, the sense of joy was almost palpable.

AUGUSTINE—ANOTHER MIRACLE

Augustine was another of God's miracles. He arrived on our verandah one evening on the tenth day of his life. His mother had given birth to him in the Government hospital at Banalia, about 15 miles (25 km) away from us. He was diagnosed as having tetanus, a common illness with the newly born, and treatment was begun on the fifth day of his life, but he became worse; the terrible spasms he had were so frequent and prolonged that his mother could not feed him. The doctor in the hospital told her there was no hope for her baby, but she wrapped him in a cloth and started to walk back to her village, resting frequently. She herself, newly delivered and carrying her load on her head and the baby in her arms, was not really fit to walk all that way in the heat of the day. Her village was one mile (2 km) further on than Bopepe, and I had been away in the city when she needed help. Now she heard I had returned and other villagers told her to come to us. She had nothing to lose by coming, as the baby would probably die in any case. So she came just as we had finished our evening meal.

There she stood, misery and fatigue on her face, and without a word she placed the baby in my arms. Mary was with me, and as I uncovered the little scrap of humanity I heard her gasp and say, 'Is that really a baby?' Augustine was like a tiny skeleton with yellowish skin stretched over his little frame, and a big unnatural grin across his face. He was in spasm and unable to cry. His eyes were open and anxious; he became blue, then as the spasm eased off his colour returned to the same yellowish tinge. His mother showed me the treatment card he had had in the hospital, and he definitely had been diagnosed as having tetanus and received the correct treatment for that disease. Now at ten days old, here he was with us at Bopepe.

What was I to do? What could I say? We all came into the living room, his mother leaving her bundle on the verandah. We explained that I was not a doctor and frankly I did not know how to help either her or the baby, but God, who was the Great Physician, knew, and he could help if we believed. We prayed together. I prayed first asking God to show me what to do, and also to comfort the mother and show her the way of salvation. Then Mary prayed, committing the baby to God's infinite wisdom and care, and as she prayed I became aware of a word going through my mind: 'Tetany, tetany', and I knew it was God telling me the correct diagnosis. Tetany is not unlike tetanus in that both produce terrible spasms, but the cause is different. Tetanus is due to an infection, but tetany is caused by a lack of calcium due to some problem with the parathyroid gland. Never before had I seen a case of it, and certainly never expected to. It was one of those rare diseases one reads about and which constitute medical history. Now here was God telling me, we had a case of tetany on our hands. Hurriedly I told Mary and left her with the mother and baby while I went to consult my paediatric textbook. I read the symptoms and they fitted exactly. I then read the treatment and my faith began to falter. Where, oh where, would I find injectable calcium in the middle of the African jungle? Why had God bothered to tell me if there was nothing I could do?

With a big question mark in my mind, I ran to the dispensary and into my little pharmacy, as I remembered that a box of samples had arrived the previous week and was as yet unopened. I rummaged through the box, and there at the bottom were ten large ampoules of calcium for injection! With a hurried 'Thank you Lord' I grabbed syringes and other impedimenta for the treatment, and rushed back to the house. According to the book and the baby's birth weight we worked out the dosage and there was enough with one ampoule to spare!

The book said it would take forty-eight hours before there would be any noticeable improvement, and we explained this to his mother. Augustine was so dehydrated he needed fluids and food urgently; the spasms were terrible to see. I passed a tube down to his stomach and gave him his first feed in five days. He was almost navy blue by the time I had finished, but he kept it down together with the tranquillizer I had added to the feed.

We housed the mother in our spare bedroom as we would need her milk. At first we fed the baby every two hours. Each time the feeding was accompanied by spasms; each time we thought he would die during the procedure. We prayed as never before. It was hard to meet the mother's eyes, they were so full of hope. How those forty-eight hours crawled by!

Towards the end of the second day the baby slept, really slept. It was true that he was being given tranquillizer, but this time his little hands had relaxed. Hastily I called Mary to come and see and we had a praise meeting then and there. The treatment was beginning to have effect.

Little Augustine began to improve daily until the middle of the second week, when he was feverish and began to cough and the spasms became more frequent and intense. Without a doctor I was thrown back on to God, for it was as I feared—whooping cough. The mother confirmed this by saying there had been several cases of it in the children's ward where she had been. By all counts Augustine should have died there in my bedroom, but by the grace and mercy of God, the babe recovered. He was in our house for twelve weeks in all and he then went to stay in a nearby village and we visited daily. During this time his mother came to know Christ as her personal Saviour, so for us it was a double miracle, physical and spiritual. I met Augustine several years later, a normal healthy mischievous boy, the pride and joy of his mother. She went on to become a deaconess in her local church.

It was at Bopepe we had our smallest baby, 1lb 10oz (750g). So tiny yet so perfect, she was a real challenge. We kept her in my bedroom to eliminate visiting by all and sundry. After twelve hours she began to cry and her tiny voice was very demanding. The daytime temperature was around 31°C

(88°F) and 24°C (75°F) all night, so she had a hot water bottle at night. The humidity is always high in Congo so that was not a worry for us.

She put her minute fist in her mouth and sucked vigorously. She was hungry and telling me! The books all said you should wait forty-eight to seventy-two hours before feeding a premature baby, but she still yelled. I showed her the book but she was not impressed, and moreover she was in my bedroom. I had had a heavy day, so I gave in to her demands and fed her. The little scrap did not look back; as regular as clockwork she wakened every three hours and was duly changed and fed. I even found myself waking every three hours without an alarm clock and did so the entire time she was with me. After fifteen weeks, she went home weighing some 5 lbs (2·265 kg). We used to call her Aggie, and thereafter all premature girls we called Aggie and all boy prematures we called Henry, regardless of their real names.

DRIVER-ANT EVANGELISM

Bopepe village was very keen on evangelism, and they instituted what they called 'Driver-Ant Evangelism'. Driver-ants are notorious in that when they invade a building, they make their presence known and felt. They clean the house of anything alive—insects, cockroaches, snakes, lizards and even animals if they are trapped. Humans do not wait; they have to move out. Driver-ant evangelism was for every able-bodied man in the village (remember, they were all believers) to go out and evangelize. They went in twos. To each couple a village was given, and like the ants they were to visit each house systematically night after night until every inhabitant had heard the gospel. Driver-ants only attack at night—hence the name for this kind of evangelism.

However, the men could not visit the kitchens, usually situated behind the house, as that was where the women sat. Therefore the women were also sent out to 'gossip the gospel' in the kitchens.

Certainly there was revived interest in spiritual things in the area, and the Bopepeites also matured spiritually too. Prayer meetings were held daily at 6am in the church. These became more lively and positive as the folk prayed for specific projects and people, and they began to see God answering prayer.

One advantage I had over my colleagues on other stations was that when a patient came in whose case was especially difficult or beyond my knowledge, the village elders were always there to pray as I worked. They would gather either in the church or outside the dispensary and pray through to the completion of the treatment. This was also a great witness to relatives too.

To get back to the prayer meetings, the villagers were very burdened for a tribe of outlaws, men and women who for some reason or other were on the wrong side of the law and lived in small scattered communities deep in the forest. The villagers had prayed much for them, that God would open the way to reach them.

One morning Mary and I were having breakfast at about 7am. We sat by the window, which gave a view of the entire village. Pastor Asani was on his verandah reading his Bible. We saw a man enter the village. We did not know him, but this was not unusual. He hesitated, saw Pastor Asani on his verandah and went towards him. We watched Asani greet him and invite him to sit with him.

We continued our breakfast when suddenly we heard Asani shout 'Praise the Lord', and then he and the man were on their knees on the verandah. By this time our curiosity was aroused and, as soon as the men finished praying, we asked our house-servant to find out what had happened.

Apparently the man had been working in his garden when he was convicted of sin in his life. The conviction was so great he could not work, and went back to his village where he told his elders. Instead of laughing at him, they suggested calling the witch-doctor, but the man refused and said he must go and find someone who would understand. He walked four days through the forest and came to a village and told them his problem. By this time he was sure he was going to a bad place, though he had never heard of hell. The villagers told him there was a village among the Bangilima tribe which could help: it was called Bopepe. It was a further two days' journey and he arrived at 7am, the morning Mary and I had seen him. He was an outlaw and had come under conviction of sin, without ever hearing of Christ, or heaven or hell. The reader can imagine with what joy Pastor Asani had led this man to Christ, and what a boost to the faith of the Bopepeites.

Men in their plantations and on the road were coming under conviction of sin and were sent to us by the local inhabitants. The harvest was beginning to ripen when the rebellion of 1964 came. Probably the battle for souls had really disturbed Satan, for during the rebellion Bopepe really suffered. It seemed he had unleashed all his pent-up fury against the village. My earlier book *Missing believed killed* tells of all that followed.

MORE MIRACLES

Another Bopepe miracle was performed the day a young woman walked into our small maternity unit. She had been in labour for two days and her case was very complicated. Instead of lying either head or bottom first, her baby was lying horizontally. The government doctor was away, and the nuns wanted to send her to the big city for an operation, but she refused to go.

After two days in labour, with contractions every five minutes, she discharged herself from the Government hospital, crossed the ferry and *walked* the 15 miles (25 km) to me. My first reaction was one of horror at her stupidity, and then of resentment that she had placed me in such a professional predicament. We tried to reason with her, and even offered to take her to our own mission hospital, but no, she would stay and if necessary die at Bopepe, rather than go a step further.

I called my aide, Mama Ruta, and explained the gravity of the case and that I was sure the mother would die. Mama Ruta talked to her about Christ and eternity. Meanwhile I went up to the house to tell Mary. It sounds silly, I suppose, but it was always a relief to explain things in English to Mary, even though she was not a nurse.

Together we prayed, asking for the wisdom we did not have. I had several books on obstetrics, and each said the same thing: 'A Caesarian section is the only answer.' That was not much help to me. Dear Mary said that God had allowed the woman to come. He had placed me at Bopepe, therefore he must know the answer. We both went back to the maternity unit, I with butterflies in my stomach. Mary said she would stay with me and give me moral support. I needed it! Mama Ruta was sent to the village elders to call an urgent prayer meeting, and they congregated outside, praying.

Suddenly I knew what to do. Because the baby was already dead, I would have to remove it piecemeal. I had never seen it done and it took me an hour to do. Mary sat with her back to me holding the patient's hands and from time to time would say, 'I can't look, Margaret, but I sure am praying.' At last the baby was removed and the mother was fine. For the first and last time in my life I heard a praise meeting going on for the delivery of a dead baby. After several days of antibiotics, the patient went home rejoicing in her delivery from danger, but more so in her new-found Saviour.

It was not all drama and miracles at Bopepe; we had our lighter moments too. My love of cats, always a source of amusement to my colleagues (and now to my friends), was known by the Africans. One day a little boy of about six arrived on our verandah with a tiny bedraggled kitten in his hands. Without a word he placed the kitten into my hands—and how pathetically thin it was! The boy pointed to his own ear and then to the kitten's. I understood, and quickly glancing at the kitten's ear, saw that it was infected. 'Do you want me to make him better?' I asked, and eagerly he nodded. I invited him into the house and he sat down, still without saying a word. I guessed the kitten could do with some milk first and gave him some, the boy watching with big eyes. Its hunger satisfied, I then cleansed the offending ear, put in some antibiotic powder and sent them away to come again in the evening. Twice a day for five days the little fellow came with the kitten, and in all that time he did not open his mouth to speak to either Mary or me, but answered questions with nods and shakes of his head. The kitten was cured, and boy and kitten went their way. I found out later that the boy was mentally sub-normal, but at least he knew the kitten needed attention and where to find it!

Mary's dog was called Simba (meaning 'lion')—an unfortunate choice we realized later on—was mainly white and needed a bath frequently. He hated them, of course, and even when Mary would say to me 'I think Simba needs a B-A-T-H' (spelling it out), he would still know and slink under her bed. When the deed was finally done, and we all got wet together, he would then dash off and roll in the smelliest pile he could find in the village!

Fidèle, our house-servant, had an aunt who had had eleven babies, all of whom had been stillborn following five or six days in labour each time. She was so bad and noisy each time that her family had built a hut for her outside the village, far enough away where she could not be heard. Fidèle asked if I would see her and help, as she was now pregnant with number twelve. It was a tall order, but I agreed to do so. She came to see me and though I had no access to laboratory facilities, I felt she was physically healthy. I explained that I was only a midwife but that God could and would help me deliver her, but she had to co-operate too, which meant coming to me as soon as she started labour. Well, she came one evening quite late, and after a time of prayer for help, I delivered her by forceps of a very lively little boy. I tucked them both up in the ward and went to bed, praising God for yet another miracle. In the morning Fidèle came early and asked me how his aunt was doing. I told him she had delivered a live baby boy. But Fidèle was perplexed, 'Are you sure you are speaking about my aunt? She only came last night'. So I sent him to the dispensary to see for himself. He came back so thrilled and we had a prayer of praise in the kitchen.

STRANGE CASES

One Sunday afternoon, we saw four men arriving at the village carrying between them what at first we thought must be a big animal. Each man held a limb and the body hung down, and to our utter astonishment they were carrying a seven-month pregnant woman who looked unconscious! Mary said, 'Looks like it's for you!' The men carried their extraordinary burden to the dispensary and I hurried out to them. The woman, or girl really, was one of my prenatal patients and also called Margarita. Her relatives said she had been vomiting and then went unconscious. Her notes showed an uneventful pregnancy up to the week before, so with a hasty prayer for help I began to examine her. All her vital signs were normal, as were all her reflexes. This was her first baby, so I wondered if there was a psychological reason for her to simulate unconsciousness. What was she trying to prove? God gave me the answer and how to deal with it.

I ordered all relatives out of the room until only Margarita and I were left. Then very quietly I told her she was alone with me and that she was please to open her eyes and tell me the problem, which she duly did.

A young wife has to move into her husband's compound and she needs to prove that the extended family loves her. Also in her case, apparently her sister had vomited during pregnancy and died. 'Please I don't want to die yet,' she ended. The fact they had brought her to the dispensary proved that they loved her and it was with quiet satisfaction I could tell her all was well physically, and the baby was fine. Then I had the joy of telling her of the Saviour and the gift of eternal life. The men came back into the room and were amazed at her transformation. We had a time of praise and prayer and Margarita went home with them on her own two feet.

Another time a group of women came with another woman being 'piggy-backed'. She had been in labour for five long days and witch-doctor and village crones had done their best, but the baby would not come. To my amazement the baby was alive but in great distress. Mama Ruta and I stood and prayed and asked yet again for more wisdom and guidance. There was only one option for me, to do a forceps delivery on an exhausted and infected woman and a very distressed baby. We explained the situation and said we had asked God to help us, but the baby may not survive. 'No problem,' they said, in effect. So we went ahead and delivered the baby. For both mother and baby it was touch and go. I took the baby to my bedroom away from all the other women, gave him the VIP treatment and he survived. The mother was very ill, but she too survived and at the end of three weeks they both went home. I still believe in miracles, for that surely was one of God's special ones.

One more strange case: One evening, just at sundown, a group of men and women came into the village with yet another seemingly unconscious girl. She had had a row with her husband (she was wife number four) and he had hit her with a chunk of wood across her head, splitting open her forehead from one eye right across to the other eye, whereupon I assume she fainted. As she regained consciousness in all the noise and confusion, she decided this was the time for the family to prove their love for her. She was about fourteen or fifteen years old, and healthy. They carried her into our sitting room and laid her on the floor.

I began to check for vital signs, especially as it was such a big head wound. I soon realized she was feigning unconsciousness, and said as much to Mary in English. So I went to the dispensary and procured all the things necessary to sew her up, but deliberately omitted the local anaesthetic. We then told all these noisy relatives to be quiet and I would mend her head, but as she was so unconscious she wouldn't need a painkiller. She was a Stoic!

Not one flinch as I put in twelve stitches, though I did say to her before each one, 'I'll put another one in', and she was prepared to enact her part. Then, the mending finished, I needed to get her back to normality without her losing face. I asked Mary if she would make a mug of coffee, add five spoonfuls of sugar and bring a spoon as well.

Meanwhile, I cleaned up her face and gave an antibiotic injection. Then we sat her up with one lady relative behind her propping her up and holding her head in place. I then explained that this (the coffee) was a very good restorative and we would give it to her by the spoonful. I touched her mouth with the spoon and each time I did so she obediently opened it and swallowed the spoonful of coffee. All this was much to Mary's and my amusement. Suddenly she opened her eyes wide, grabbed the mug and promptly drank what was left. Shortly afterwards they all departed and we restored our sitting room to tidiness. Giggling, we rehearsed the whole incident. The girl made an uneventful recovery, and her belief in her many relatives reassured. Such are the social life and traditions of a Congolese village.

MORE ABOUT VILLAGE LIFE

I well remember one evening showing Mary a crack in the floor (it was a cement on earth floor). Then we noticed that day by day, the crack grew wider until we had to move furniture. Two days before Christmas, when we got up in the morning, the crack had widened almost 12 inches (30cm) in the night. While we were having breakfast the entire wall, extending from our dining area to the lounge area and incorporating two windows and a door, fell outwards on to the verandah, leaving us very exposed to the road and the village. Missionary visitors who called in that day on their way up country, had two little girls with them. The five year old looked at the pile of debris and our wall-less room and remarked in the understatement of the year, 'Oh dear! You do have problems, don't you?'

As it was dry season we could not re-mud the walls or make cement, so the villagers put thin branches in the gaps and filled them in with the long banana leaves. As the leaves dried, so we became more visible to all and sundry. Ultimately the rain came and we had a mud-making day.

Mary used to love making bread, and once a week would make eight large loaves. I would come home from the dispensary and see eight loaves all without their end pieces (or heels). Mary would say, 'Oh honey, I just couldn't resist them just out of the oven.'

We were living in a village community and so we were involved in the lives of our neighbours. One late afternoon we heard the noise of someone approaching our house, and there to our amazement was a small boy of about ten years, with a saucepan over his head and face, being led by his very irate mother with a rope round his neck. They were followed by the children of the village and some of the mothers, all shouting at the boy, 'Thief! Thief!' The boy understandably was crying. A loud knocking on our door and the mother presented the boy plus saucepan to us, saying, 'This is what we do to children who steal food.' Apparently he had seen the food in the pot, eaten all of it, but was caught red-handed. It was harsh treatment, but he never stole again. He had to go to every house in the village before they took the pot off!

We had made friends with the government doctor from Banalia hospital, and he and his wife would visit us or vice versa when time allowed. One day the doctor turned up with another man who was introduced to me as a doctor from the World Health Organisation (WHO) in Geneva. He was doing research on government and private dispensaries in Congo, and had come to inspect my department. The Africans had built me a cute dispensary, with a waiting room and maternity unit. It had mud and wattle walls, a cement floor, copper mosquito netting at the windows and a leaf roof. There was also a long building made into three two-bedded rooms, with African type beds (called karagbas) and two kitchens (or mafikas) for relatives to cook food. I was so pleased when he said it was the happiest and cleanest and tidiest one he had seen. The Africans were rightly proud of his comments.

There is one incident which recalls the odd view the locals had of us, or of me in particular. My hobby was keeping chickens, ostensibly to supplement our diet, but I found I was also supplementing the diet of a dog from the next village. Noticing that my eggs were getting fewer, and even the eggs under a broody hen were disappearing, I tried to keep watch, and then one day I caught the dog in the act. He was eating an egg right outside the hen-house. We called his owner, who went by the grand name of Hezekiah, and complained about his dog who had the unfortunate name of Mokile-Mabe ('Bad World'). Hezekiah said he would take the dog hunting with him the next day, which he did.

I had been up all night and then had to work all morning in the dispensary and was late home for dinner. Finally I arrived back at the house at 2.30pm and found Mary and Pastor Bo waiting for me. Bo said that Hezekiah was on the verandah with his dog and they wanted me to 'mend it'! Mary was adamant that I had something to eat first, and while they argued I looked at the dog. Poor thing! He had flushed out a gorilla; it had turned on him and had torn open his throat, including the trachea (windpipe). It had also gored his sides, and they expected me to mend it! Even now I know next to nothing about the anatomy of any animal. What was I to do? This wretched dog who had stolen my eggs was looking at me with big soulful eyes and wagging his tail. Once more I explained I was not a veterinary doctor, but I would ask God to show me what to do, as he had created the dog and would know where I had to sew. So we all prayed, Bo, Mary and I. Then I told Hezekiah he would have to pay the full rate of expenses incurred and he agreed. He carried the dog to the dispensary, and first putting a bandage round his muzzle, I proceeded to mend the dog. All the time I worked I talked to the dog, who kept up his tail-wagging, even when I must have hurt him. When I put the last stitch in his trachea, to my astonishment and delight he made the whinnying sound dogs make when they want to get attention. So I mended the dog and carried him up to our house to sleep there for the next six days. He made an uneventful recovery but never barked again. However, while I worked on the dog, Pastor Bo was talking to Hezekiah and the outcome was that two weeks later he found Christ as his Lord and Saviour!

When President Kennedy was assassinated in 1963, we first heard it on BBC World Service at 10pm—and Mary, being American, was galvanized into a flurry of activity. She suddenly headed off into the village, knocking on doors and shouting at anyone who would listen that her president had been killed. Frankly, they were not interested and it was left to me to try and console her. She sat up all night listening to bulletins on the radio—I callously went to bed.

A MOUSE'S NEST IN THE FREEZER

I will end my saga of life at Bopepe with the story of yet another answer to prayer. It was Christmas Eve 1962, and when we got up that morning it was to find the fridge-freezer had defrosted overnight. It ran on kerosene and we knew it was full as we always refilled it and relit it every Saturday. But try as we would none of us, Mary, Fidèle or I, could get it to relight. We had bought supplies to cover the holiday period and it was completely defrosted. Even the butter was runny! So we prayed and asked for wisdom as we did not know what had gone wrong. Then we had breakfast, and about an hour later we heard a truck pull into the village and stop outside our house. Who should get out but Hector McMillan of Bongondza! He was the 'Mr Fix-it' of the mission, his motto being, 'If it is difficult I can fix it, and if it is impossible it might take a little longer.' What was he doing on Christmas Eve at Bopepe?

Apparently he always gave his wife chocolates at Christmas, and when he was last in town and needing to buy supplies and collect his six sons from school for the vacation, he had forgotten to buy chocolates. He had left home at 6am that morning, arrived at Bopepe three hours later for a comfort stop. When we poured out our dilemma to him, we said he could have all the chocolates we possessed if he could fix our fridge-freezer. His jacket was off almost before we finished speaking (it would save him eight to ten hours more driving) and he found the trouble. A mouse had built its nest in the flue, which had completely extinguished the flame. In less than an hour the fridge was running perfectly, he had more chocolates than he could have hoped for, and as we drank coffee, we had a praise meeting.

The way in which God engineered that episode was a real boost to our spirits. The fridge had defrosted, Hector McMillan was three hours away worrying about the lack of chocolates for his beloved wife, and it all culminated in a joyous praise meeting. How good is the God we adore!

MISSING, BELIEVED KILLED

Our time at Bopepe came to an abrupt end when Congo, and notably our corner of it, was engulfed in a very bloody revolution. Mary and I were arrested and imprisoned, but after several weeks I was released back to

Bopepe as I was British. Mary, being American, was not released. Two days later as events escalated, Mary and other missionary prisoners were murdered, as related in my previous book *Missing, believed killed*.

I was made prisoner again and miraculously rescued several months later and returned to the UK. As it was not possible to return to Congo for another year, I was seconded by UFM to work with the Sudan Interior Mission (SIM) as it was then known, at Galmi Hospital in the Republic of Niger for that year. I was then able to return to Congo.

Missing, believed killed

For readers who are not familiar with the author's harrowing experiences at the hands of the Simba rebels, here is a short resumé of the events recounted in her earlier book, *Missing, believed killed.*

The 1950s were turbulent years for many African nations which had not yet been granted independence from colonial oversight and government, and the Belgian Congo was no exception. While, in some nations, local African leaders were being trained to take over government, this was not so in Congo. After riots had taken place in Leopoldville, then the name of the capital city, the government began to lose control over both the economy and the military situation. Thus in 1960, Belgium agreed to the handover of power—but there were few local Africans with the necessary experience to run the country smoothly. The result was that there were a few years of extreme turbulence and these included the mutiny of the army, the repatriation of foreign workers, and large waves of civil unrest.

Margaret returned to a shattered economy, rapidly deteriorating dirt roads and neglected plantations. Educational institutions, both schools and universities, were failing. And so it was that in the middle months of 1964, a rebel army was formed, and it seized power in the north east of the country where Margaret's mission was based. Thus began the Congolese Simba revolution of 1964. Many of the rebels were boys as young as nine or ten years old.

Margaret's eight-month ordeal is well summed up in the words 'Missing, believed killed', for there was no direct knowledge of her whereabouts at the time. She witnessed the murder of a number of her colleagues and associates.

Brian H. Edwards has written:

'Margaret's own story has long needed to be re-told for a generation that was not yet born when she was a prisoner of rebels in the Congo, and for eight months was missing, believed killed. She will protest that it was not her personal faith but the One in whom she placed her faith that brought light into the cruelty of those terrible months. This is a story of the God of miracles and of the reality of the presence of Jesus Christ with his people in the darkest nights of human cruelty.'

The full account of Margaret's ordeal is to be found in *Missing, believed killed*, and an extract from one of the chapters entitled *Nurse—prisoner of the rebel army* is to be found at the end of this book.

Banjwade

After a busy time at home and in another country with another mission for a year, we, that is Olive McCarten and I, came back. Olive too had been caught up with the revolution in another area but had escaped the massacre. She was released and rescued at Christmas 1964 and returned to the UK. She and I came back to a heart-warming welcome and then after a few weeks the time came to settle down into what hopefully would be a normal term—if missionary life could ever be called normal. Exciting and exhausting, yes, certainly challenging and at the same time we were learning to trust more and more in God and continuing to be amazed at how he engineers circumstances and at times does a miracle to keep us humble and awed by his power, surely cutting us down to size.

Banjwade was one of the original places where UFM worked, and before the rebellion of 1964 had a flourishing Bible School, primary and secondary schools, a busy dispensary and a very active church. We came back to a place where all the buildings were in a sad state of repair; the water system had broken down, and there was no electricity. The houses were in a filthy state with damaged walls and windows, plus the debris left behind by opposing forces. The church was still standing, but the roof had numerous holes caused by bullets and when it rained during a service we either used umbrellas or moved.

The staff was very depleted. At first, Barry and Ruth Morris and their four children, Jean Raddon and I were the entire complement. Jean and I set up house together. Fidèle and his wife and family, known to us from Bopepe days, came to join us.

Barry and Ruth were from the UK. Barry was an evangelist and preacher as well as a maintenance man. Ruth was a nurse who eventually taught in the Bible school as well as caring for her children. Jean Raddon, also from the UK, was a teacher and head teacher of the secondary school. Initially Barry was kept busy trying to keep abreast of the many repair jobs needed, and he also managed to get the water system running, which was no mean feat. Jean and I managed to repair our house both inside and outside, though we let Barry do the windows. We bought locally made furniture, but we had proper beds and mattresses—a necessity when nights were frequently disturbed.

Shortly after our arrival at Banjwade my baggage arrived and with it a brand-new operating-cum-delivery table, and two glass topped trolleys. These had been a special gift to us donated by friends in my home church, East London Tabernacle. I knew these ladies had given sacrificially over the years I was in Congo as well as before and during furlough. When I tried to explain this to the Africans, they would not believe it was from ordinary people, some just on pensions; they insisted they must be wealthy people. It made me realize afresh that to be wealthy is a purely relative term. Even as we gave thanks for the table, the glass topped surgical trolleys and other instruments, I smiled as I thought of my friends, wealthy by African standards and rich by Christian standards. Those items of equipment were to be used hundreds of times to save lives and to usher in new lives.

We were kept busy preparing for our ongoing ministries, and finding national staff. Once the schools and the Bible School started, the place was a hive of activity. In the dispensary was a trained male-nurse, Leon Abende, and he was the recognized head nurse. At first I went along to help him, then as the maternity work developed, I helped when I had time. He used to send all his gynaecological problem cases to me and I sent him my medical cases. Thus we worked as a team, each supporting the other; we picked each other's brains and learned a lot, at least I know I did.

Bombalisi Moise was the dispensary and maternity evangelist. He was a polio victim and in those early days 'walked' on hands and knees, for the rebel soldiers had destroyed his invalid chair. His knees had large calluses on them. Through the mediation of Kinso (our previous field director) and the kindness of Oxfam, we were able to get him a self-propelling invalid chair. He was an enthusiastic worker and, apart from illness, he was always on time and ready for his work. He preached most of the time in Kimanga, the tribal language of that area. The staff would meet for prayer each day before the beginning of clinics, and we took it in turns to lead. In the course of three and a half years we had many answers to our prayers, and although the normal routine continued, things happened which enlivened or saddened our days.

DELIVERING BABIES

I began prenatal clinics and we announced them with the drums. Fifty women attended the first clinic, and I thought that was a good attendance. However, it took me well into the afternoon to record case histories, take blood and do all the usual examinations. I had taken on two aides who had worked there before the rebellion, and a Christian midwife named Lucia Maway, who had worked with me at Bongondza before her marriage. These ladies helped a lot in the clinics, and certainly were indispensable for their smooth running. The numbers increased until we were having 120 a session.

At first I was alarmed at the widespread evidence of anaemia. It seemed that fifty to sixty per cent of normal was their 'normal'. We did not give blood transfusions simply because there was no blood, and in reality nobody could afford to give a pint, except maybe the missionaries, and few of them had high blood counts after they had been in Africa for a couple of years. So we relied heavily on iron tablets and injectable iron when it was available, and then only if the lady had received treatment for hookworm (which was endemic in Congo) and if her blood count was less than forty per cent of normal. Many times I thought of our clinics back in Britain, the treatment we give, and the lectures we had showing the dangers of anaemia in pregnancy and delivery. It did not help to dwell too much on these things, for I had to work in a God-given situation and it was surely a triumph of his grace that in all my years in Congo doing obstetrics, only one mother died from anaemia.

On several occasions a woman would be desperately ill following delivery, and I knew of several whose blood count would be down to twenty per cent on the third day. During these crises we were thrown upon the mercy of God, and on each occasion we were able to obtain valuable, but expensive, iron injections. The patients paid what they could afford. I was guided by my staff in this, for every African pleaded poverty to me; I always believed them and they knew it. So my staff would find out each patient's financial status and they paid accordingly. Even so, I hated taking their money.

It is a grim, inescapable fact that in the bush areas, the lot of women is a hard one. They were hard at work from sunrise to sunset, seven days a week. The only time a woman ever had a vacation was after a baby was born and she would go then to her mother's village for two or three months, sometimes longer if her husband had more than one wife. Even when staying with her mother she would be expected to help with the chores. Small wonder then that evangelistic work among women is hard going, especially with their being away from home, or unable to pay attention owing to chronic anaemia and with the added factor of being tired physically after hard work in the garden or a long walk in the heat of the day. Nonetheless we did see souls saved, though often it would be after the husband had been brought to faith.

Infant mortality was high, and after asking a patient how many children had she borne, I always followed it with 'And how many are alive today?' Few had all of them alive, and those who did were invariably Christian women who had utilized the medical services of the mission. Many women had lost half the number they had; and others still more. One had had seven stillbirths in a row, another had delivered ten babies but only two were alive. I do not think I ever really became hardened to these facts, though seemingly on the surface it did not bother the women; but surely to see eight little graves must have some impact on the subconscious mind of the mother?

Somebody asked if the folk came to utilize our services quickly, and the answer is both 'Yes' and 'No'. It is not a case of setting up shop and being assured of custom. Certainly we can be highly qualified professionally; eager to meet the local people, care for them and present Christ to them, but not all Africans are impressed by qualifications.

By the time I arrived on the Congo scene, the spadework had been done and missions and missionaries were accepted as part of the general scene. Even so, we had to be accepted as individuals by the local population. Very few missionaries go out already fluent in the language and so the study of this and the culture go hand in hand. During this time the African watches; very little passes him by.

They watched how we lived, our attitudes to fellow missionaries, our attitudes to the local people and with respect to the latter they were understandably very sensitive. Once one had made friends with them, even though the language was still a barrier, they would watch the work the new person did. Whatever work may be assigned, and in my case it was in the medical role, if the local people saw that one was competent, then word would be passed around.

The Lord was pleased to use me in miraculous ways in obstetrics and word soon spread. It did not matter that I would have been very happy not to have done any midwifery at all, but as God used my hands to save lives, so more and more people came, and I ended up doing eighty per cent midwifery and only twenty per cent general nursing. For someone who only did midwifery training for status and who hated every minute of the training, it was rather a reversal of affections. No doubt God knew what would be ahead of me and organized my training days.

I have wandered far from whether the Africans came for help quickly or not. Usually the Christians would come to us straightaway, but the unbelievers would consult the old wives, the witch-doctor, and often these would charge much more than we ever did, and only when all these failed did they come to us. By this time the case was usually out of hand; they had come too late for us to help, but if we were successful, next time they would come straightaway.

Yes! We also saw miracles at Banjwade. I can still vividly remember a day when we were thrown back on to the mercy and grace of God as we sought his aid. I had admitted a woman in labour who was haemorrhaging very badly, and the situation was quite simply desperate.

It was a Sunday, which in a way made it worse, for we did not use our radio transceivers on Sundays, which meant that I could not contact our mission doctor. Ruth Morris, whom I had contacted for help, went to her house where the radio was installed and called any doctor who may have been listening. There was no answer. Half an hour later still no answer, but eventually at about 3.30pm she had an answer from a doctor at Oicha, about 600 miles (950 km) up-country. Ruth explained the situation and asked his advice. His first suggestion was to get the patient to hospital. That was out of the question; she would never survive the journey over our terrible roads. His second suggestion was to do a Caesarean operation, but we did not have the equipment (let alone the knowledge). The third was to turn the baby and deliver it as a breech birth (it was already dead anyway). Time was running out for the patient too.

We prayed with the patient, having explained what we would do, then continuing in prayer, we gave her an intravenous injection to put her to sleep, and we were enabled to do the impossible. The baby was stillborn as we anticipated, but the terrible haemorrhage stopped. God heard our prayers and the mother's life was saved. Ruth kept her rendezvous on the radio two hours later and let the doctor know the outcome.

Those radio transceivers are worth every penny spent on them. They maintained vital contact with our other stations and were almost our lifeline with the outside world. Certainly at times of crisis it was such a help to be able to speak to someone who could help, be it a medical or a business matter. Maybe the folk in town did not appreciate it as much as we did, for they would then get all the messages and have all the running around to do, whereas before, the missionaries had to go into town and do their own shopping.

A WEEK OF TRIALS

One particular week stands out for me. It was August 1970, towards the end of the month. It was a Tuesday, and Viola Walker, a veteran missionary in her early sixties, was trying to clean a window of her house. She stood on a clump of earth, which suddenly crumbled and she fell heavily, rolling down a slight incline away from the house. Somebody picked her up, placed her on her bed and then sent for me. I was just about to begin my Tuesday clinic. Poor Viola was in a lot of pain and quite blue, and it was obvious to me that she had fractured the head of her right femur (thigh-bone). Everybody was talking at once and dear old Viola was lying there so patiently with never a murmur.

The radio came into its own that day, as we summoned aid from the big city. In the meantime, we had to care for Viola and ease her pain. Actually the folks did not arrive until the following afternoon, as some workmen who were working on a large bridge refused to allow them to pass until it was time to finish work. By this time it was 3pm. It was with relief that we saw Viola go, not to be rid of her, but to know that she would be in good hands. We had delayed an injection of morphia, so that we could give it to her immediately before the journey. She must have been in considerable pain, but I do not remember her complaining. An American doctor in town operated and it was touch-and-go, for Viola almost died on the table. Unhappily, the wound became infected and the pin was out of alignment. As a result, Viola was flown home to Canada in the care of Betty O'Neill.

But there were more trials to come for us at Banjwade. That same week, on the following Sunday, we had invited Jean Schlegel (a new missionary from the USA) to lunch and afterwards we separated for our siesta. The afternoon meeting was cancelled for some reason or other, but Jean had forgotten and had gone to the church at the correct time. As there was nobody there, she went home by another way. We had seen her earlier as she had passed our house, and because the drums had not called we were still in the house.

In the evenings on Sundays it was our practice to get together as missionaries for a time of fellowship in English at 7.30pm. Jean was late, but as she was generally late we did not worry, and we gave her five more minutes. At this time there were only four of us: Pat Olds (a UK missionary), Jean Raddon, Jean Schlegel and I. After five more minutes we decided to go and find her, but just before the time was up, someone came to our door and said they thought there was an ill person in Jean's house, but there were no lights on and only strange noises coming from it. Taking a small hurricane lamp with us, Pat, Jean Raddon and I went to Jean's house. It was just as the Africans had said, except that by now lots of people were standing outside her window and door. The noise came from Jean's bedroom but we could not identify it. We called her to open the door or window, as the house was locked. Finally we broke a pane of glass and let through a small boy to open the door. I guess we had not spent more than a few minutes in all this.

The three of us entered her bedroom; Jean was lying on her bed, under her mosquito net and in her pyjamas. She was making weird noises almost as though she was laughing and crying at the same time. She then put three fingers into her mouth as though to try and vomit—or was it to try and breathe more easily? We shall never know, for she stopped breathing. Quickly we put her on the floor and tried to resuscitate her, but she never breathed again. She was with the Lord. The time, 7.55pm, was just ten minutes after we received the message. She was only twenty-four years old and had been in Congo just two months from America, to teach in the secondary school.

To say we were in shock puts it mildly. We hardly knew how to pray. All we could do was repeat over and over again, 'Oh Lord, Oh Lord, Oh Lord.' We did the last offices as we do at home, and would have turned out the light and locked the door at least for the night, but this was Africa and we had to bow to culture. Their way of mourning is different from ours, and the body is left on view to receive the respect of the population. We compromised a little by covering Jean with a sheet leaving just her face and shoulders uncovered, and we, as chief mourners, had to sit there all night, looking at her, while the local Africans came and went. I think the little bedroom was full all night, yet they came and went maybe every half-hour.

As soon as I had realized Jean had died, I scribbled a note, in retrospect terse in its brevity and gravity, 'Banjwade, Sunday 8pm. Jean Schlegel has died, please come quickly', and I signed it. We sent the note with a man who had a bicycle. The hours of watching and waiting were agony; we were still very shocked and unable to cry. I think the Africans could not make us out. We could only pray and cling to the Lord, acknowledging his sovereignty and that he never makes a mistake. Jean was at the very beginning of her missionary career. Was all that training wasted? Obviously it was her willingness and obedience God wanted, for he does not really need us, though it pleases him to use us. 'What I do thou knowest not now' (John 13:7). One day it will all be clear to us, but by that time it will not really matter.

The cyclist arrived in Kisangani. Four US missionaries, Del and Lois Carper, and Thelma and Marshall Southard who had only arrived from furlough the day before (Sunday morning), were having breakfast together. We can only guess at the consternation the message caused. It must have been after 8am, for Lois went to the radio to try and contact us. We had tried practically on the hour every hour from 5am, and at 8am there was still no response. At 9am we tried again, heard Lois, and quite unpredictably the tension broke and we all began to cry. Pat regained composure quickly and told Lois all that had happened. They promised to be with us by mid-afternoon, as they had to notify the American consulate and the Mission's Home Board. They also had to arrange for an autopsy.

During the morning the Africans identified with us. They brought flowers and a nucleus of Jean's would-be students came and sang so beautifully and tenderly. Now that the tension had been broken and we wept, so did the Africans. I did not know at the time that a message had gone out on the drums, telling women in labour not to come to the maternity unit that night. I had wondered why no one came, and in fact was hoping one would come to relieve the tension of a long and painful night. But as always the Africans were so thoughtful.

The staff from the city came with a coffin. This time the workmen on the bridge let them through. We learned that Jean had died from a violent allergic reaction (anaphylactic shock) to the malarial prophylactic drug which we all take. The drug she was in the habit of taking did cause these reactions from time to time: I had seen it in the dispensary, mostly with children. The car carrying the coffin was decorated with flowers by the Africans. As word was passed by the drums that the car was en-route, it was very moving to know that villagers stopped their work and lined the road outside their villages. Jean was buried in the Kisangani cemetery, the same place where many of our martyrs from the 1964 rebellion were buried. Her death drew us closer to the Africans. It also helped us to understand something of the depth of sorrow the Africans experience when they lose someone suddenly, as happens all too frequently in the villages.

Opposite to us across the road lived a large family. The husband was an ex-pastor who was out of fellowship because of his adultery. He and his wife cared for their numerous children and one grandchild. The grandchild was a boy, about three years old and the bane of his grandmother's life. He could be heard screaming, fighting, protesting most days, so that one day when I was talking to him I told him I called him 'Kelele' which meant 'noisy'. Somehow this had an effect upon him, for wherever he saw me thereafter, he would come up to me, putting his hand in mine and ask rather wistfully, 'I'm not kelele any more, am I?'

One day little Kelele became very ill and within twenty-four hours he had died. I was shocked. I went to the house, which was packed with grieving villagers and relatives. I sat with them for about forty-five minutes just looking at the now silent form of the child. Just to sit with the mourners was identifying myself with the family in their shock and grief. But how I missed that little fellow! Part of our identification with the Africans was to participate at times like this in the various customs of village life whether or not they were similar to ours. Both Jean and I sat with the villagers at each death, as it meant more to them than any amount of preaching. We both also attended funerals, work permitting.

I was interested in the Africans' appreciation of music. As a rule, our classical music is not understood and therefore not appreciated. Therefore you can imagine my delight when one day as I was feeding some babies in the house, I played a tape of Christmas carols. On it there was a new rendering of 'The First Nowell' by a boy chorister, who had a voice like a bird. The notes came tumbling down from the roof of the cathedral, like the notes of a lark. I was enthralled, and was so taken by the sheer beauty and unusual quality and tune I played it over and over again. Our house-servant Fidèle had been washing dishes one day as I played the tape, when I became aware of him standing in the room with me. His face was rapt in wonder, tears were trickling down his cheeks and when the song finished he confessed that he had goose-pimples all over, so beautiful he had found it to be. I tried it again on the schoolboy who did our ironing, and he almost burnt a hole as he put the iron down to listen.

LIGHTER MOMENTS

Light relief was found in our pets. Three of us had cats, all of which became pregnant at the same time. It was very amusing one day to go to the bathroom cupboard and find Ruth Morris's cat on the lower shelf having her kittens. The next day Jill Thompstone's cat wandered into my bedroom and had her kittens in the box I had prepared for my cat, and both ladies were puzzled as to why their cat had come to my house, but I put it down to feline wisdom. Although they were both nurse/midwives, I was the only midwife in practice! Incidentally, my cat had her kittens unattended as I was called away at the crucial moment to attend a human birth, and on my return she fixed me with a baleful glare and showed me her kittens.

Dentistry is a job I would rather leave to the men, but it often fell to my lot to do extractions. At least I had received some instruction through the Christian Dental Fellowship before I came to Africa. One day, I had a very difficult male patient who had an acute bladder problem, and after relieving the acute condition (but not the cause) I happily sent him to our doctor at Bongondza on a truck going that way. Imagine my consternation when later that same day a Land Rover pulled up outside our house and out jumped our own mission doctor. He wanted a tooth out and would I do it? I was scared. It is one thing to pull a tooth for someone who doesn't really know me, but quite a different thing to do it for another who is experienced in the art, and a doctor into the bargain. I asked Leon if he wanted to do it if I held the doctor's head, but he said he would hold his head and let me do the extraction. We set the instruments out on our dining-room table. Word soon got around and the window was crammed with inquisitive schoolboys. I warned the doctor not to make a noise because of the audience, and he manfully allowed me to pull his tooth for him! Then half an hour later, he got into his Land Rover and drove all the way home, a journey of several hours.

Life in the jungle is often enlivened by the nocturnal visits of driver-ants. These creatures, about half an inch (15 mm) long with pincer-like jaws, swarm all over the house in their thousands, their target to eat literally anything which is alive. We had been regaled by senior missionaries about these ants' propensities, and were always warned to move out when they move in. Unhappily they are very nocturnal in habit, so frequently folk are in bed when they arrive and a sharp nip from their vicious pincers may be the first intimation of their arrival.

One night, Bess, the Morris's dog, which was staying with us, wakened Jean by her whimpering at midnight. Jean, being wise in the ways of dogs, listened and responded to the dog. Bess's ears were pricked forward in the direction of our chicken house, which was just outside her window. Jean could hear the hens squawking and the chicks cheeping, and shining her flashlight she could see the driver-ants swarming! A yell to me and we hastily lit lamps. Our main objects were two-fold: firstly, to release the hens and chicks and, secondly, to place a barrier between the house and the ants. There was no time to lose.

It really was an hilarious time. One of us would hold the lamp and the other would make mad forays into the chicken house, which was smothered with literally thousands and thousands of hungry ants. The hens without chicks flew out into the moonlight, but those with chicks stayed put, gamely trying to pick off the ants as they invaded the nests. My job was to rescue these 'families' (they were, after all, my hens and my hobby). Imagine us jumping up and down (for the ants travel fast), running into the house with a handful of chicks and a distraught mother hen, the other taking them and placing them in buckets. From time to time we changed places, in order to pick the ants off ourselves. We became almost hysterical with laughter; in fact we laughed so much that we impeded the work. However, we succeeded in rescuing the hens and chicks and somewhat belatedly began preparing our barrier around the house when Jean called out that they were already in the bedrooms.

A house opposite was empty as the Morris family was on furlough, and we took the dog, cats, kittens and premature babies over—in that order (which shows where my affections lie!). We arranged the hens on the backs of the dining-room chairs, the chicks in baskets on the table, encircled the table with creoline (a strong creosote-based disinfectant) which the ants will not cross, then abandoned the house. By this time it was 2am.

Jean was up first and went to the house at first light. The ants were lined up and moving out. We were not prepared for the chaos which presented itself, not least that the hens had all turned round on their new perches, and we needed to scrub the chair seats as well as the floor surrounding them! The smell was lessened by the large amount of creoline we had used. All this was just another night in the life of a missionary living in the jungle. We praised God that no harm had come to babies or pets and our house was clean from insects and lizards for a little while.

MILK JUST IN TIME

Most of our work was routine, but from time to time God gave us little miracles. One such day occurred in the early days of our work in

Banjwade. A baby girl was brought in by her grandmother. She was grossly underweight and very dehydrated. Her grandmother had rescued her when the baby's mother died in childbirth. She had somehow managed to procure a baby's feeding bottle and had made a teat from the inner tube of a bicycle wheel. Bottle and teat were filthy, the milk was sour and had clotted, the baby was hungry and almost too weak to cry. She also had appalling diarrhoea, which was not surprising. In one sense I was afraid to take her into our house in case she infected the other frail baby residents, but felt led by the Lord to admit her and keep her in my bedroom.

We used to have a supply of milk from the American government, so with a new bottle and teat we made up fresh feeds. The baby drank hungrily; at least there was nothing wrong with her appetite. She had one bad habit: she would cry when left in her crib. Grandmother had always carried her about, but she really was too ill at this stage, and there was no lessening of the terrible diarrhoea. She used up our store of diapers in no time, and we were hard put to meet the needs of all the premature babies.

Obviously the American milk did not suit the baby—it had additions like extra iron and vitamins—and the only solution was to buy a large tin of full-cream milk from Europe. The cost was prohibitive on a long-term basis. Grandmother had no money and my allowance was already stretched to the limit. So we prayed and told God we needed help as soon as possible. The very next day I received a letter from headquarters to say that money had been deposited into my account 'to buy milk for any orphans'. How perfect was the timing of this gift! The letter had taken ten days to come; truly it was another fulfilment of God's gracious promise: 'Before they call, I will answer' (Isaiah 65:24).

The baby responded almost immediately to the new milk, stopped crying, and there was no more diarrhoea. She began putting on weight in a couple of days.

Two days later we were able to teach the grandmother how to prepare feeds and keep the bottle and teat clean. Thereafter, she always travelled with a tin of milk, a small saucepan kept scrupulously clean, and a clean bottle and teat. The supply of money for the milk never dried up, the little one was fully weaned by eighteen months, and I last saw her a healthy little three-year old, equal to her peers who had had the advantage of being breast-fed. In addition, grandmother had heard the gospel daily.

From this last case we had the opportunity of taking on many orphans and supplying them with milk and bottles, and the supply never ran out. Always when we were down to our last case of milk, more money would arrive, enabling us to build up our stock again. Milk came in large 5lb (2.5 kg) tins, always in powder form and easily mixed with water. Where we lived there were no cattle and therefore never any fresh (liquid) milk. How faithful God was in supplying this very special need. Each day was committed to God in prayer, and it was always inspiring at the end of the day to see how God had engineered our activities.

FOUR BROKEN LEGS

Once, when Olive McCarten had come to stay with us for a few days, during one afternoon a call came for help from an area about 3 miles (5 km) away. There had been an accident involving three policemen, a truck and a car. We hurried to the scene and found the three policemen (one was a superintendent), and all had broken legs. We made the truck driver take them back to Banjwade.

After examination, we found the superintendent had broken both legs and the other two men, each had one broken. As we could not care for them at Banjwade, we sent a runner into the city on a truck which was passing, to inform the hospital to expect the injured. We went to the workshop and appropriated three long planks of wood. We splinted the men on them, (from head to foot, poor dears) and gave them morphia. With much prayer and trepidation, we set off on a nightmare journey of 25 miles (40 km) into the city. Olive was driving a Bedford van and the men were laid side by side on the floor of it.

The road was treacherous and, even driving slowly, it took all Olive's skill to avoid the various large pot-holes in the road. We finally arrived at the hospital at 7pm, having taken three hours to cover the distance. The men were Stoics and did not complain at all about the pain and discomfort. We happily unloaded the men on to the waiting stretchers, planks as well—we never did get our planks back. We were able to arrange for one of our men missionaries who lived in the city to visit daily, and all three made uneventful recoveries.

NIGHT VISITORS

Night calls were an established part of my routine, though I never got used to getting up in the small hours and always had a little grumble to myself as I dressed. At first I used to hear people call me, but as exhaustion took over from tiredness, it was Jean, more often than not, who would hear and then she would call me. I always felt so guilty about it as Jean was always late to bed, but not once did I ever hear her complain about being disturbed. In fact on several occasions I would come back to the house about 3am to find Jean sitting in our living room with one of the premature babies in her arms, soothing the hungry little mite with love, as she was not sure how much feed to give. The baby would have wakened on time and begun to cry and Jean would get out of bed to comfort him. It was so gracious of God to allow me to share a house with Jean.

Clinics were held four times a week, two for expectant mothers and two for babies and under-fives. Once a month we did medicals for the school children, though these were really Leon's responsibility, and I would help if I were free.

All clinics were preceded by a gospel message, prayer and hymn singing. Numbers varied with the time of year, For example, if it was the time to plant peanuts, the numbers would be low. Again, if it was wet we did not even hold clinics, as most folk did not possess raincoats or umbrellas; indeed, some did not even possess a complete change of clothing. Responses to the messages were variable, though seldom a week passed but that someone wanted to 'turn his heart'. The women's clinics and baby clinics were the most difficult, for invariably the children were a distraction. They are not disciplined until they are two years old, and given several lusty voices it could be a veritable fight between preacher and audience.

Living in a clearing in the jungle we accumulated quite an assortment of livestock in our homes, such as lizards, frogs, insects, ants and cockroaches (the latter being the bane of my life). Spiders, big and small, were also everywhere. We had one new lady missionary (who will be nameless) who went to bed one night, her mosquito-net tucked in all around. Suddenly she saw a large spider in the corner of her room near the ceiling. She screamed several times, causing two of us to rush to her house expecting to find some great trauma, and there she was sitting up in bed, pointing to the spider, which was quite happily having a rest. It didn't take too long for the lady to become accustomed to spiders and even snakes.

DYING AND DEATH

An African funeral is a very sad affair, as are all funerals, but judging by European standards it is psychologically more healthy. Their method, while seemingly more crude, is in the long run more beneficial and cathartic. The body is placed on view, usually in the largest room of the house. Someone is delegated to move all the joints every half-hour or so to prevent them from stiffening. Villagers, families, and friends all congregate in the room, there being a constant movement to and fro as some leave and others take their place. Wailing is long and loud, and tears really flow, the immediate relatives being longest and loudest in wailing. Christian families tend to cut down on the noise, but the tears are still there—and why not? All this is usually accompanied by various off-noises, depending on the wealth of the family. If they can afford it, a rough coffin is made on the premises and the sawing and hammering creates a mournful background to the wailing.

Someone will have collected money and bought a piece of cloth and some perfume. When word comes that the grave has been dug and the coffin finished, the body is lovingly washed, dressed, perfumed and placed in the coffin, if there is one, or otherwise in a hammock, and taken to the graveside. Each village has its own burial site usually a ten or fifteen minute walk into the forest. According to the religious beliefs, so the body is buried. A Christian burial has a similar service as we would have in Britain, while a pagan one is minus prayers and hymns, and extra things placed on the grave, for example some plates, a lamp and food. When the body is lowered into the grave, usually the nearest relatives go berserk and need to be physically restrained by several strong men. Yet, when it is all over, life goes on as normal with little if any protracted grief, and I certainly have never seen anyone mentally ill following a death in the family. In fact they will often discuss the whole affair twenty-four hours later and even laugh about it, while we Westerners would still be in a state of shock.

One day Leon, one of our African nurses, had treated a child in the dispensary. The little one had malaria and Leon had given her an injection, when ten minutes later the child collapsed and seemingly died. Leon came running to me in the maternity unit and while he prepared an injection, I began cardiac massage and at the same time instructing another aide to do the 'kiss of life'. Leon gave the injection, and then did the only other thing possible—he prayed. It seemed all the people were holding their breath except the mother who by this time had begun to wail. We worked on for ten minutes (or was it only five?). It seemed like an eternity to us, when suddenly the little one began to breathe, at first just a shudder, then regularly and her colour became normal. She opened her eyes, took one look at me and screamed for her mother. The noise and rejoicing which followed was almost beyond belief, but Leon and I could only give praise and thanks to God for another miracle, but at the same time I secretly wished God would be less dramatic!

Another time Leon came to me to ask for help; we had several boarders at the school on the compound, and apparently following a dispute between two teenage boys, one boy cursed the other, resulting in the boy who had been cursed falling down unconscious. His friends carried him to Leon in the dispensary, and Leon called for me to help. This was a new one for me! We prayed, asking for wisdom. Suddenly I knew what to do. Checking the boy for signs, I realized he was not unconscious but only feigning it, but he needed to frighten his opponent and at the same time not lose face himself. I asked Leon to find some liquid quinine (if you have ever tasted it you will know that it is very, very bitter). Watched by half the school, I poured a generous 10 ml into his mouth, at the same time saying, 'In less than five minutes he will wake up and ask for a drink of water.' We did not need to wait five minutes, for he sat up immediately and drank nearly two pints of water. Cured! Thank you, Lord, for your help and guidance in such an odd situation.

PREPARING TO RETURN TO BRITAIN

My last day on duty before returning to Britain on leave was a memorable day. We had a lady who had a history of six previous stillbirths, and her baby was due that week. I had told her to come in for an induction on the Monday if she had not gone into labour. God ordained she should go into labour on the Sunday. When I examined her I knew she was in for a tough time. We prayed together, asking for strength for her and wisdom for me. As labour progressed I realized she would have to have an operation, and frankly I was scared. I went back to the house and reread my textbook, but it did not alter the picture. I pleaded with God for wisdom and physical strength to cope with the situation.

We explained the gravity of the case to the young mother who gave me the go-ahead. We prayed together, committing us all three into God's hands; the mother, the unborn baby and me. The operation is one used often in under-developed countries, and involved making the pelvis larger in all its internal dimensions. I had learned how to do this when working in Niger. The procedure happily resulted in the safe delivery of a lovely fat baby girl, who screamed her protest at such an entry into our cold world. Due to extensive bruising of the baby's face, we kept her in our house for twenty-four hours while the swelling went down. The mother was delighted and, as we prayed together afterwards, she wept.

This birth took place at a time when Christian names were not being allowed by the state on pain of imprisonment. Nearly all adults had to revert to a tribal name at this time. As I filled in the baby's birth certificate the mother said the baby was to be called 'Margarita'. I called her husband, and explained the name would be wrong, but he just reiterated the name was to be 'Margarita'. When I said he could go to prison for it, he drew himself up and said, 'Even if all three of us go to prison, that is her name.' So my time in the country ended even as it began, with a baby called Margarita.

A few days later, packing finished, and goodbyes said to all my dear Congolese friends, I was ready to return home for an indefinite period to care for my mother.

When the car came to take me to the city, a group of Congolese Christians came, stood round the car and sang, 'God be with you till we meet again' in Swahili—all six verses and choruses! It so happens I have not met them again, at least not here on earth, but undoubtedly I will when we all get to heaven.

UK Interlude

Coming home to care for my mother was a painful experience emotionally, for I loved Congo and the Congolese dearly. If I am perfectly honest, I was resentful. Because I was the only unmarried daughter with a career in the family, the other three being housewives who went to work, I was expected to give up my career and look after Mother. From my point of view, this was terribly unfair. I took all my complaints to the Lord. He reminded me that he was sovereign and he had it all under his control. Then events began to move, and within two weeks I had a job along with accommodation. My training would be useful, and I would get extra training in social work.

Mother flew in from New Zealand where she had emigrated, and she moved in with me. I was forty-seven years old, and retirement was a long way ahead, so I prayed that if Mother died before I retired, I would go anywhere God wanted but, 'Please don't send me back to Galmi Hospital in Niger.' The local church I attended had three ex-missionaries, all of whom had come home to care for their mothers. One mother was ninety-one, another ninety-four and the third was a hundred-and-one. My mother was only eighty! Could I last the distance?

It was not an ideal situation. Until she came to live with me in Central London, Mother had always been within easy distance of several family members. Now, with three sisters in New Zealand, one brother in Africa, another in Jersey and the other two in the Home Counties, all she had was me. My unsocial hours of work created problems, not insurmountable ones, but requiring much grace daily, and of course the Lord gave the grace as needed. Eventually, I obtained a job in Surrey and we moved to a small house, but even further away from the family.

This time my local church was Hook Evangelical, part of the Fellowship of Independent Evangelical Churches, and Brian Edwards was my pastor. I attended when duties permitted and became a member several months later in 1975. Earlier that same year, three months after we had moved in, Mother became very ill and died seven weeks later in hospital. During that period I had signed a contract for two years, working for Surrey County Council.

GOD'S GOOD GUIDANCE

A lot of people talk about coincidences, but as Christians, we believe that nothing happens by chance, so what happened next?

Mother died at 4.30pm on a Saturday. Next day, being Sunday, I went to church in the morning. Brian Edwards was preaching about the life of Joseph, and came to the place where the butler promised Joseph he would speak to Pharoah about him, but he forgot. Brian then made the comment that so frequently we promise God something and equally frequently, when the crisis is passed, we forget. As I was driving home after the service, and thinking about the sermon, suddenly I realized that God was reminding me of my promise to go anywhere if Mother died before I retired! The thought hit me so hard I had to pull over and stop the car. 'But God,' I said, 'Mother hasn't been gone twenty-four hours yet.'

The next day, a letter came from SIM Galmi Hospital. It had taken ten days to come, and what did it say? 'We are asking if you would be willing to return to Galmi and develop the obstetric work.' 'But God,' I said again, 'Mother hasn't been gone forty-eight hours yet.' There was no let-up. Two days later I attended the midweek service and there was a missionary speaking on 'The fields are white unto harvest but the labourers are few.' I know I did not need to tell God we had not even had the funeral, but I did.

Several weeks later, I attended the evening service at church and Brian Edwards said something like, 'You allow your possessions to come between yourself and God.' Well, I did not have too many possessions and was grateful for what I had, but when I went home, my two cats came running to greet me and to rub against my legs. I said, 'Oh Father God, I've had these two cats for three years. Do I have to give them up?' The answer came back immediately, reminding me that God cares for the sparrows and he was perfectly able to care for two cats. The final word came the very next day: I went to my hairdresser, and as she placed a towel round my neck said, 'My husband asked me to ask you. If ever you go back to Africa, may we have your two cats?'

In the interval between these episodes, I had written to Galmi Hospital in answer to their letter, to explain that I was under contract until 1977 and I would be in prayer before making any definite decision. One day I was thinking about all these things, and not being sure what to do, I prayed asking God for one more specific word from him. I even dared to 'put out the fleece' like Gideon (see Judges 6:36-40), and to me the answer would be receiving a letter mentioning Africa. Of course the letter came, didn't it? The very next day, the postman brought a letter from a friend I had not heard from for months. There was a postscript right at the end, rather as an afterthought: 'When are you going back to Africa?' Couldn't be clearer, could it? Frankly, it was a relief to capitulate and say to God that I would go back to Galmi, provided they still wanted me there.

Knowing from past experience that it takes almost a year from applying, being accepted and going, and feeling positive that God could quite easily shut the door, I applied to SIM and said I could give them ten years, if they still wanted me at Galmi Hospital. God was very patient with me as I dithered, half hoping they would say no but almost sure they would say the way was still very open.

So it was that I went for an interview, and was accepted then on the spot. Galmi Hospital it was to be. I shared the news with my pastor and the elders and they were very happy about it. There was still a year to go before the end of my contract, but things were put into motion. The deputation work and shopping were all done. I had all my injections, a visa was obtained, and finally a date for leaving was fixed. How quickly that year went and God yet again and again met every need as it arose. His promise all those years ago had been, 'My God shall supply all your need' (Philippians 4:19). I think we frequently underestimate the power of God especially in practical things. So what happened then?

Having been back in Britain for five years I had acquired various things, and I was wondering what to do with them. I found a copy of the Yellow Pages and was looking under 'Storage', asking God to show me to whom I should apply, when there was someone at the door: none other than Brian Edwards! He had come with an offer from the deacons and elders to store my things in the roof space of the church (at that time there was roof space) where it was warm, dry and insured. Embarrassed, overwhelmed and hardly able to believe what I was hearing, I pointed to the Yellow Pages and explained what I was trying to find out! Yet again God had stepped in at the precise moment of need!

A month later, with just a week to go, I once more opened the Yellow Pages to find where I could hire a van to move my things to the church. I am sure you will have guessed by now. I had another visit from Brian Edwards to say that three men from the fellowship would come with a van and take the things to the church. I got the feeling God really wanted me to go to Galmi Hospital.

The morning came to leave, the men came as promised. My next door neighbour, up to then my deputy, took the morning off to help, and his wife provided tea and biscuits. My neighbour, who was a Moslem, watched in wonder as three happy men did all the work, no swearing, no snide remarks, no complaining and finally he made the comment that Christian men were very different from his friends and that he was so impressed. I praised God for this final token of testimony.

And so, exactly two years after signing a contract, within a couple of days of its expiry, I was on a plane en route for Niger and Galmi Hospital, secure in the knowledge that it was in God's will I should go. The future was in his hands.

9 Galmi Hospital in Niger

I actually spent two different periods in Galmi. However, for the sake of explaining about life as a missionary I am going to blend the two periods, as what appertains for one is equally the same for the other. There was a ten-year gap between the two, but hopefully the difference will become evident as the events recorded unfold.

So to Galmi in the Republic of Niger. This is a landlocked country in North West Africa, part of the country is in the Sahara Desert, though Galmi is on the southern border of the desert known as the Sahel. Need I say more? There is a dry heat most of the time with two per cent humidity during the nine month dry season and eighty per cent humidity during the three month 'wet' season. There is very little rain even at this time. The hot season runs from March to June, when the temperatures soar to 55°C on most days and it is only slightly cooler at night. Between December and February (the cold season) it is much cooler, with daytime temperatures down to around 25°C. At this temperature we thought it was freezing. I was impressed by the sand, the blistering heat, the cloudless sky, the cold nights and early mornings, the stars at night and the glorious moonlight. In Congo our horizon had been the tree tops; in Niger it was uninterrupted, and sunrises and sunsets were wonderful.

FIRST IMPRESSIONS

First impressions tend to stay. I was fascinated by the camels, with their ornate trappings, also the horses and the almost ubiquitous donkey: none of these animals lived in our part of Congo. To see the men dressed in flowing robes was just like a Bible picture come to life. Some, but not many, of the women were veiled. Poverty was just as obvious, maybe more so than in Congo. Owing to lack of water the people did not bathe so frequently, so there was an aroma to which one became accustomed after a short while.

The usual crowds were there, only the feel of the crowd was different. Invariably in Congo the crowd was with you, whereas in Niger they seemed to stand apart, rather like 'them and us'. These were the people God had sent me to work among and to love for his sake.

The hospital was built by a veteran missionary, Doctor Burt Long of the USA. He had begun the work, with his own team of nurses, eighteen years before my arrival. Now the hospital 'in the middle of nowhere' was on the map. Thus I would be working with a large team instead of alone (medically speaking) and usually with two or more doctors. This was so different from Congo.

Burt took in every kind of patient: surgical, medical, children, obstetrics and gynaecology, genito-urinary, tuberculosis (both pulmonary and bovine), and of every nationality and colour. The man was seemingly tireless. Always busy and overflowing, the hospital, built to take 120 patients, invariably had 170 or more depending on the season. There were cases such as camel bites, people who had been struck by lightning, amputations and fractures, tetanus and meningitis. These were all dealt with, apart from tropical diseases and women having babies.

The system was simple enough. Patients who were very ill slept on a bed and as they recovered and more ill ones were admitted, they transferred to a mat on the floor. Being called at night meant negotiating one's way down the ward, and it was to me always an occupational hazard, for the lights were dim and bodies would be lying everywhere, made worse by the fact that each patient had one relative staying with him or her.

Outpatients was a colossal department, with numbers sometimes up to four hundred attending in one morning. The first group would be in the all too small waiting room, and numbered tickets were given out as the folk came in. When a hundred had gathered, the door was shut and the evangelist or missionary would hold a short service. Meanwhile the staff would finish their last minute preparations. Then one by one the patients would be seen by missionary nurses. Those cases which were simple enough would be ordered treatment. The rest had to wait in another room for the doctor, who would be operating, trying to beat the heat. So it would go on throughout the morning. Sometimes it seemed as though the crowd would never thin out, but of course it did. As my knowledge of the Hausa language was nonexistent at first, I was only able to help with treatments, mostly injections and pharmacy. Once when the laboratory missionary was off sick, I was able to work there, my training in Belgium coming in very useful.

My work was ostensibly obstetrics, but in the Muslim community there wasn't too much to do, as the husband rarely allowed his wife outside the house even if she was in difficulties. In the first year I was there I only had about seventy or eighty cases. These were frequently very difficult and because of the primitive conditions in which the women lived, the complications were such that even text books did not make mention of them. The complications were such as are never seen in the Western world with its good antenatal screening. To me they offered a challenge on the professional level, but during that first year when I could not speak Hausa, the spiritual challenge had to be left to colleagues. It was always sad to see a mother die in childbirth, so unnecessarily, too. Always there was the 'if only'. But we were there to evangelize, not to Europeanize.

The infant mortality rate was high too. It did not take long to find out that a mother did not breastfeed her baby for the first four days. In their folklore it was said to be bad for the baby. Consequently the baby, who would be hot and hungry, was fed condensed milk or contaminated cow's milk, usually from dirty containers. Thus the baby developed gastro-enteritis very quickly and died a few days later, if it survived long enough to fight off the effects of the 'native medicine' given on the eighth day.

Another interesting but sad custom is that where the mother has borne her first baby, she does not look at the baby or show any pleasure. She is afraid to show affection as the child might be taken from her as soon as weaning is over, again always supposing the child lives that long. The heartache of these women is tremendous for I cannot believe there are many women in the world who really do not love their babies. The need of the gospel is so evident, and the task is huge; who is sufficient for these things? Obviously we are not, but God is, and he would give us grace and wisdom daily—how we needed it!

JOS IN NIGERIA

Just a month after my arrival in Galmi, we heard on the radio that a plane would be calling to take me to Jos in Nigeria. I only had one hour's notice to do everything, so I tidied the house and packed a case. The difficulty was knowing how to pack, as I had no idea why I was going, or for how long. At midday I was taken to the airstrip 10 miles (15 km) away to meet the plane (several years later we had our own airstrip at Galmi). Only then we heard that an orientation course had been fixed lasting two weeks, and as a new missionary to SIM, I was to be going to it. Jos is a busy city in Northern Nigeria, several tribes converging upon it. To me it was the largest mission compound I had ever seen; whole streets of houses were occupied by missionaries.

The course was helpful and it was of interest to see how very little difference there was between our missions (namely UFM and SIM) in policy, also the similarities of culture between the Africans in Nigeria and Congo. I made many new friends, both new missionaries as well as veterans. When the two weeks were over, I flew back to Galmi and quickly settled into the routine.

GALMI AGAIN

One Sunday I was able to visit a local village with one of the missionaries as she went to follow up hospital contacts. The heat, flies, dirt and poverty remain in my memory. The tremendous spiritual need stands out too. The difficulty in getting the message across was so great and there was a great need for repeated visits. There was an abject lack of missionaries to carry out this urgent task.

Services were held in Outpatients daily, and the wards were visited by missionary staff who were off duty as far as their hospital work went. They went from bed to bed, but the noise and distractions do not make the ward an ideal place for preaching. The men's ward was more difficult; the women listened readily but usually had several children to distract their attention. Though most were nominal Muslims when at home, illness tends to polarize their thinking about God and how to placate him, so they were very rigid in their rituals several times a day. In these circumstances, evangelizing is hard work and seems to bring little results. All operations were preceded by prayer, usually by the doctor, and all deliveries were ended by prayer.

In Niger, as in all Muslim communities, the baby receives its name on the eighth day with the ritual killing of a ram, prayers and feasting, and in Niger the baby's head is shaved completely for the occasion. I never did get used to seeing the babies thus shaved, for usually they were born with a mop of silky black hair. The Christians did not follow this ritual, though normally they had a feast on the eighth day.

Wednesdays were market days, and after lunch two of us would go to buy meat and any odds and ends available to supplement our diet. The market was visible for miles, owing to the presence of the vultures, which would be flying overhead. The meat part of the market smelled and one had to be careful in buying any. Meat was relatively cheap but always tough. Unhappily we expatriates were always followed by a crowd of children, who vied with each other to touch our skin, or they would crowd round so tightly we could hardly move. It was sad to see the donkeys and camels hobbled and standing patiently in the hot sunshine, with no food, water or shade in the 'donkey park', which was the equivalent of our car park. They frequently had sores on their backs, all covered with flies. The mission did not have permission to have a stall in the market or to preach there. Nevertheless, it would have been an ideal place.

Life in Niger is never boring. One day I watched one of the nurses prepare an enormous syringe with penicillin, only to find it was for a camel who was patiently waiting outside the hospital gates.

A missionary who travelled on horseback was going on a month's vacation and my next door neighbour, an American nurse, agreed to care for the horse, so one day I came home and found an enormous horse tethered outside my bedroom window. A little shack had been set up a few yards away made of corn stalks and he stayed there for a month. By the end of the month he had half-eaten the walls and the roof! I was getting used to sleeping with a stable smell when his owner came and rode him away.

I always thought frogs lived in damp climates, but they also live in the desert. We had an outside lamp on the verandah, and consequently the moths and other insects would be attracted to it, literally by their hundreds at night, and there sitting on the ground waiting for them to fall would be anything from twenty to thirty frogs. Maybe it was their idea of McDonald's with free frizzled moths on the menu. I did not mind the frogs sharing the verandah, but when they moved into the house I did object—not that they listened. They would be everywhere where it was dark and cool. When sweeping the house, I became used to frogs leaping over the broom and scuttling back to the dark recesses under the furniture. I felt a bit like Pharaoh when Egypt suffered the plague of frogs. Happily the wet season only lasts three months each year.

Sunday services were hard to sit through at first. Not yet knowing the language, I found it hard to concentrate. As in Congo, the men sit apart from the women. They always leave their shoes outside. The services could be restless. The local person, not being used to wait for convenient times, would just get up and walk out of the service to relieve himself. This meant people had to move to let him out and then again when he came back. At one service I attended, there were twenty-five excursions outside and back during the sermon. Maybe I should not have counted but it really fascinated me. One really needs to pray for extra grace and inner calm when attending. It does help though, when the language has been learned.

Another time a local person was preaching and his son of about nine years was misbehaving in the front row. To my astonishment (but no one else's), the preacher left the platform, still preaching, boxed his son's ears still preaching, then still preaching went back to the platform as though the incident had not happened.

LIFE IN NIGER

Life is hard for believers in Niger. They are often denounced by family and friends, and frequently turned out of house and home. They come to the mission for work, but there is a limit on how many people can be employed, especially when it is unskilled labour. A missionary's income is limited too, and salaries for house-help can be very high.

Our day began officially at 6.30am with a prayer meeting. This necessitated getting up at 5am in order to have a quiet time with the Lord and drinking a cup of tea. As it is dark until 6.30am we had to light a lamp, but later on we had electricity which was a great boon. The prayer meeting would last until 7am, and then the night staff would give their report. We then rushed back home for a quick breakfast and came on duty by 7.15am.

Before we had all-day electricity (and therefore air-conditioning), most operations needed to be done before the maximum heat of the day at about 11.30am. The doctors operated five days a week, not on Thursdays or Sundays apart from emergencies. Between them I have known them do as many as four major and six minor operations before noon. The nursing staff gave the anaesthetics.

One Thursday, as we were doing our mid-week clean up in the operating rooms, I was called by someone to go to the main entrance of the hospital. There was a Land Rover, and my identity being established, the driver opened the back and pulled out a fully grown ram. This was a gift for me from a grateful patient. Very kind of him and all that, but what would I do with a ram in the desert? It was decided to kill him and divide him up between us all. I had only just lived down all the teasing the gift provoked, when, lo and behold, two weeks later another Land Rover arrived with yet another ram. He, sad to relate, met the same fate as the first one. In Congo I could have kept him, as the vegetation was lush, but in Niger there was not a blade of grass. I have always regretted we had to eat them.

SPECIAL CASES

It was at Galmi I dealt with my very first case of gas gangrene. A woman who had been in labour for six days had been treated at a government dispensary, but she could not deliver and because of malpractice in the village had developed gas gangrene. There was little we could do to help her physically, but I was able to ask a missionary nurse to go and talk with her, and the poor woman found peace with God before she died a couple of hours later. It was lovely to hear her say she was going home to God, whereas previously she had been so afraid to die.

Another case comes to mind as I write. One morning as I came on duty and was passing through to the men's ward, there was the unmistakeable smell of gangrene, so I followed my nose and found a young boy of about ten years crouched down in a corner. He was whimpering and holding his left arm across his knees. The smell was appalling (probably that was why he was on his own), and he had come in the night to wait for us. His arm was swathed in rags and I wondered what was underneath them. As I undid the rags and came to the last one, I realized his hand was black and as I removed the last rag, to my horror his forearm came away with it, leaving a piece of bone protruding just above what should have been his elbow! Apparently a camel had bitten into his forearm, and the local orthopaedic witch-doctor—yes! sometimes they 'specialize'—had applied a splint made of sticks of wood, but had bound it so tightly that the circulation had been cut off. The upper arm was grossly infected and the smell intolerable. Hastily we gave anti-tetanus injections and that morning he underwent surgery to amputate most of the upper arm. I was the anaesthetist on that occasion. He made an uneventful recovery. Incidents like this were not at all uncommon.

The 'ambulance' was often a camel, and once we had a man, who had a broken back, brought in on a camel. Needless to say, he died a few days later.

Tuberculosis was very prevalent in Niger and the hospital had a clinic twice a week, to weigh patients and give injections and pills. Most of the patients were men who lived in a separate compound at the back of the hospital. It was uphill work teaching simple hygiene, like instructing patients to spit into a container rather than on the ground. The clinics were opportunities for presenting the gospel in an unhurried way and usually with continuity as the patients would be coming twice weekly for several months.

Because of the high cost of drugs, we had to fix a price for treatment, and it would often be that a patient could not afford to pay. The sad result of this poverty was that he would not present himself for treatment. Consequently, he would infect his family and the sorry story would go on from generation to generation.

One man wanted to earn money for treatment and had the bright idea of selling guinea-fowl eggs. These eggs are small with a hard shell and keep well in a refrigerator for up to three months, provided that they are fresh at the start. My next door neighbour rashly told the man she would buy any eggs he brought. He began with five, next day he brought ten, next day two dozen, finally ending up with whole sackfuls. I guess the guinea-fowl population was reduced rapidly in that area! Poor Martha became desperate. We all bought eggs from her until our refrigerators were full. One day I went into her house and she showed me her refrigerator; there was layer upon layer of eggs! I felt guilty and went to my house to make more room in my own refrigerator for eggs, but even then I ultimately had to call a halt. I assume the man managed to pay for his treatment. All I know is that we had to stop the unending supply of eggs.

The national food in Niger is different from that of Congo. With little or no vegetation for most of the year, millet was sown and harvested during the three months of the rainy season. This grain was the base of the diet, cooked and pounded into grey-brown cakes and eaten with gravy. Locusts dried and smoked were a delicacy and although I didn't like them too much, I would eat them if offered by a local person. At least they were a source of protein.

The men would eat first, whether at home or in the hospital, and it took me some time to get used to them sitting in the ward, facing the wall, because it is very bad manners to watch people eat; it is just not done.

One day in the women's ward, I noticed a small group of grey-haired ladies sitting around a tiny wind-up record player. They were listening to a record from Gospel Recordings (a US organization) made in their own tribal language of Buzu. As they listened I sat with them, not understanding a word, but praying that they would understand not just the words but the meaning.

The record was played through a second time at their request. They were fascinated by the voice coming from the little yellow box, and as it played the second time, they anticipated the general context and listened closely. At the end they remarked that they were 'good words'. For the third time the record was played and this time they listened with their whole concentration. As the preacher asked questions, they hastened to answer him. A quaint picture? A group of old ladies talking to a gramophone? Not really. I am sure incidents like these could be multiplied many times.

Living as I had in Congo with its lush vegetation and bountiful fruit, I missed this in Niger. Most of our shopping, apart from meat, was done by post and by the time the vegetables arrived they would be small and dried and hardly worth the money. Butter could be bought from the market; it was always runny because of the heat and often had a few flies floating in it. It was but a simple matter to strain the butter, boil it, and then put it in the refrigerator. Not really up to Western standards, but it made a change from the inevitable margarine bought in tins.

Because of dust storms I needed to keep my radio and alarm clock in plastic bags. The storms could be seen approaching as a long brown cloud away on the horizon. Everyone would then run to close windows, shutters and doors. As the storm approached, usually within five minutes, gale force winds would precede it and it was not uncommon to see someone's roof gliding through the air as though dancing in a macabre ballet, and the trees bending almost to the ground. The dust would rise and in a few minutes it would be almost dark, and all one could do was to sit it out. If caught out without shelter, a local person would crouch down and cover himself with his cloth, curled up like a hedgehog, until the storm abated. Then, when it had passed in ten to fifteen minutes, and the rain came, one summed up the damage, and swept out the home of the inch or so of dust which had blown under doors and between the cracks. In the hospital, beds and floors had to be swept, but somehow we all managed to take this in our stride.

CHANGES IN CIRCUMSTANCE

After one year in Galmi, I left to go back to Congo and work what turned out to be my last term there (recorded in chapter five). Then I went back to the UK, caring for my mother until her home call. Thus ten years elapsed before I returned to Galmi (chapter six) at the insistence of God, the invitation of the SIM and with the full backing of my church, Hook Evangelical Church, in Surrey. Up to now I have recorded incidents which occurred in that first year. When I returned, the cultural mores had not changed, and as far as I know they are still unchanged.

There were some changes, however, on the hospital compound. The supply of electricity was more constant day and night, and an internal telephone system had been installed. There were more staff, both national and expatriate. At that time, I was the only person from Britain, though there were others from Europe and Australia as well as America and Canada. More houses had been built, together with a small swimming pool and a tennis court. Outpatients had been moved to its own new purpose-built block, together with the laboratory and the X-ray department. The X-ray machine was a vintage model, but it worked!

By this time, the airstrip had been moved from its distant location to the back of the compound. My previous next door neighbour, Martha Simm (an American missionary), came to the airstrip to meet me and gave me a very warm welcome. She had also found a small ginger kitten for me, which we promptly called William. I had been allocated a small semi-detached house designed for singles, and I moved in lock, stock and barrel. The only drawback was that the new airstrip was just a few yards from my bedroom window.

After a few weeks, I had a break-in to my house one evening while I was at the hospital. When I came home, little William was sitting outside the front door looking very frightened, with all his fur puffed up to make him look bigger. As I went in, there was chaos everywhere! The thief had dispossessed me of all my linen, cutlery, radio and cassette player as well as some food. Once more taking the spoiling of my goods joyfully (see Hebrews 10:34), I was able to pray for the thief. So I began my time at Galmi with borrowed linen, cutlery and radio and cassette player.

Not knowing the language of Hausa was a problem, as most patients and staff did not speak French. So it was decided I should go to the language school in Nigeria for six months. There was some opposition to this, but the visa came and eight months after my arrival I went to Nigeria with another girl from the hospital who was Swiss. By this time I was fifty years old, and needed God's enabling, and he gave it. One problem I had was with pronouns: they were similar or the same as in Swahili, but used in a different order, so I needed to pray for God to remove Swahili from my brain, which miraculously he did—permanently! After six months, I managed to pass the exams. It really takes two or three years to be fluent, but I knew enough to get by, and fluency came slowly over time.

It was good to understand what the patients and staff were saying, at least most of the time. I was able to start taking prayers with the department staff before we began work in the mornings.

In the six months I was away on the language course, all but two of the previous expatriate staff had gone home, and I was one of the two who were left, so practically all the staff were new to me. Many had returned from furlough or some had transferred from other stations either in Niger or Nigeria. Also, while I was away, there had been an outbreak of hepatitis among the expatriate nurses and Martha had to be flown home. Her house was empty. I moved in, and it became my home for the next eight years.

The hospital had engaged a charming local midwife named Rahamu. She had trained in Nigeria and spoke fluent English. Amazingly, she was still single at the age of twenty-one. A keen Christian, she turned down a lucrative offer of marriage in order to serve the Lord in Galmi. It was joy to teach her abnormal midwifery and in some cases we learned together. Eventually she did marry one of our laboratory technicians, but stayed on all the time I was at Galmi.

Later I was joined by Heather Barrow, a nurse/midwife from the UK, and Dawn Summers, also a nurse/midwife from New Zealand. That made four trained staff, and we ended up with eight aide-midwives all trained by us, all Christians and all but one married with families, the families continuing to increase. However, as the staff increased in numbers so did the work load, and frequently we midwives were doing shifts of twelve to fifteen hours.

One amusing episode stands out in my mind. It was the hot season, and the ward had twenty-eight women, all newly delivered. Each had her own thermometer at the head of the bed in a pot on the wall. The aides had been round and taken temperatures, so I looked in the book for the records for the day, and to my consternation every patient had a temperature of 40°C. With visions of a ward of very ill post-natal women, I went to see them, but they all seemed normal, and no one complained of feeling ill. Certainly none of them *felt* hot, though the ambient temperature that day was 50°C. Then I realized the problem! I had taught the aides how to shake down the thermometer when the patient returned it, and this they did religiously, and put each individual thermometer back into its own little pot. The solution in the pot was of course at room temperature, and consequently each thermometer rose to the highest it could record, 40°C. Thereafter we kept them all in the refrigerator between times.

On the compound we eventually had thirty different households, and at one time we had nine different nationalities, each with its own particular culture. It was a joy to enjoy fellowship with one another and learn from one another. There were such diverse cultural groups as: Japanese, Korean, Taiwanese, Chinese, Swiss French, Swiss German, French, German, New Zealand and Australian, American and Canadian and British, yet we all had this oneness in Christ. In a special way God was so precious to me, for even in the times of utter fatigue when I found it sometimes too hard to pray, it was with wonder and trust I knew he would understand and would be there all the time. It was also helpful to know that my many friends at home were praying for me; I will never know just how much they helped.

DEMON POSSESSION

As our expertise improved, so the abnormal cases seemed to arrive, but God in his mercy gave us all the wisdom we needed. Sure, we made mistakes at times and learned the hard way. But God gave much grace at those times too. On one occasion I was in the ward office and could hear shouts and screams coming from the ward. An aide came running and said one of the patients was demon-possessed and out of control. Not thinking what to do next, I ran into the ward to see a girl throwing herself about on her bed, screaming and shouting, and her relatives standing there unable to touch her. With a quick 'Lord, help!' I ran to her bed and in English shouted 'In the name of Jesus Christ the Son of God, get out of her, how dare you come into a Christian hospital!' Suddenly all was quiet and the girl laid back on her pillow, utterly spent. I found I was trembling so much that I had to sit down. That was the only time I had ever had to confront real demon-possession, and I too felt utterly spent, but what a privilege it was to be used in that way by God. It made me understand more of the times we read of Jesus being weary. Physically his earthly ministry was strenuous, but spiritually he was constantly up against intense opposition from Satanic powers.

WATER!

It was in my second term at Galmi when a French firm came to drill a well. They worked three shifts of eight hours each day, and brought with them noisy and powerful machinery. It so happened that the ideal place for the new well was only thirty yards from my bedroom window, and the loud and persistent percussion boring went on sixty times a minute for almost eight weeks until they reached water. I was on night duty and would fall asleep to the regular crump, crump, crump sound and found that I only wakened when they had occasion to readjust the machine when a sudden silence would descend. When the water was reached it gushed powerfully out of a pipe and folk from the town, and, of course, the children came to bathe, play or collect water. The water was warm and soft. What a boon the water was! It was sufficient for the hospital, the compound and for parts of the town. My house being near the beginning of the pipeline, the water was a constant 40°C, just right for showers and washing. We really praised God for this extra blessing.

Also in returning for my second term, it was good to find that men from Nigeria, just over the border, were selling fresh vegetables and would come round to our houses to sell.

In Niger, it is often the lot of the younger boys to shepherd the goats, collect them in the morning and take them to a watering hole. These boys were very young, maybe eight to ten years old. One morning, when I was off duty, I noticed a large group of goats milling around outside the perimeter fence separating the airstrip from our houses. The young shepherd boy was sitting down watching the goats. It was, very hot, as usual, so I went out to the boy and asked if he would like a drink. His answer endeared him to me. He said, 'I would like some water for this nanny-goat, as she has just had her kid, and we are resting until she is able to go on walking'—whereupon he picked up this tiny newborn kid and cradled it, watched by its mother. Of course, I supplied water for him and his goat. To me this was an object lesson, showing the tender care we have from the Good Shepherd.

At the entrance to the airstrip were two oil drums side by side, with a plank of wood across them to form a seat. On the wire fence above this seat was a crude sign saying, 'Galmi International Airport—Transit Lounge.' Well, it is serviced by SIM Air, the air arm of the mission and the personnel were truly international. Frequently we would be near the 'Transit Lounge' area to wave folk off or welcome them in.

Reading through many of my letters, I notice the frequent mention of missionaries arriving for short or long term and missionaries leaving for furlough or for good, end of term or retirement. It meant a fluctuating team with which to work and called for much adaptability from all of us. It also meant we had to learn to 'let go' when particular friends left and we realized that in all probability we would never meet again on earth. This is never easy, but God would give the necessary grace to cope with the immediate loss, though one never really got used to it.

I can remember boarding the SIM plane at Galmi with four primary school children who were going to Nigeria to boarding school. At the airstrip the mothers were weepy, the fathers less so, and the children were clinging on to their mothers. I thought I was in for an emotional trip but, to my astonishment, once we were airborne the children stopped crying and were playing games with one another, laughing and joking! Heartless creatures, I thought. The poor mothers were having a good weep back at the station, and probably wept for hours.

As I began to lose my hearing, I became more sensitive to people with any degree of hearing loss, and God used that sensitivity when we admitted a profoundly deaf woman in labour. Her relatives spoke to her with the sign language they had developed over the years. Her mother told me that she had became suddenly deaf when she was about two years old. They had paid many witch-doctors but had obtained no help. The woman was about eighteen years old and had been admitted in labour with her second pregnancy. I was curious and felt God nudging me to investigate the sudden cause of deafness. I checked her ears with an auroscope, an instrument with a built-in light used for looking into ears, and to my amazement saw something blue where the ear-drum should be. I checked with one of the doctors and he confirmed my findings. As I explained what the mother had told me, he too became very interested, and offered to check the woman under anaesthetic.

It was all very exciting. A blue button was removed from one ear and a bead from the other ear. It just seemed so unbelievable! We waited excitedly by her bedside as she regained consciousness, and when she did she clapped both hands over her ears as she heard sounds for the first time for sixteen years! We needed to put in some ear plugs at first until she became accustomed to the loud noises around her, and believe me they were loud, as the family and friends rejoiced with us. I felt it was so gracious of God to use my impending hearing loss to restore the hearing of a young mother. Only God could have engineered the sequence of events to effect this miracle, and we gave him all the praise and glory.

During my time at Galmi, we dealt with so many abnormal deliveries, but none more so than three sets of Siamese twins, all within eight months. Sadly, the two sets I delivered were dead before delivery, and Heather delivered the third set, but they were premature and only survived an hour. The first set I delivered, the mother actually ran away, fearing the evil spirits whom she thought had caused it.

APPROACHING RETIREMENT

Eventually time caught up with me, and retirement was imminent.

I had begun in primitive conditions, relatively speaking: no running water, no telephones, no electricity or machines which used electricity, and in those conditions proved God's all sufficiency. Gradually things improved, and by the time I left, there was electricity twenty-four hours a day, air conditioning, running water twenty-four hours a day, telephones and fax machines. Shortly after I left, the e-mail network came as well.

The new missionary of the 21st century has different problems and stresses, but God is unchangeable and fully able to give grace and sufficiency for whatever may come their way. However, the human race remains unchanged, in need of the saving grace only Christ can give, no matter where folk live and under what conditions.

As for myself, I can only testify to a profound sense of gratitude to God for his patient dealing with me over these years. All praise and glory to his name!

How true are the following two verses from the Scriptures:

'"For my thoughts are not your thoughts, neither are your ways my ways," declares the LORD' (Isaiah 55:8 NIV).

'"For I know the plans I have for you," declares the LORD, "plans to prosper you and not to harm you, plans to give you hope and a future"' (Jeremiah 29:11 NIV).

Retirement

LIFE BACK IN ENGLAND

Before leaving to go back to Niger from furlough in 1981-82, I had an interview with my pastor, Brian Edwards, who enquired regarding my plans for retirement in four years' time. I have a feeling that I once again said I had prayed about it, and thought God had it all under his control, and I would wait and see how he would organize it. After all, it was still four years ahead. Time passed all too quickly, and I had one year left before leaving for retirement. A letter came from Hook Evangelical Church enclosing a photograph of a ground floor maisonette situated only four minutes' walk from the church, and that the church were thinking of buying it for my use. What a surprise! I was thrilled but embarrassed and humbled before our sovereign Lord who could do this for me, when I had been so reluctant to go to Africa in the first place!

In 1986 I returned to the UK and moved in the day I arrived, into that very same maisonette. Coming back to live permanently was quite different from being on furlough (or home assignment as it is now called). For the first time it would be without a family home, as both my parents had died and siblings were married and dispersed either in New Zealand or elsewhere in the UK, and they had their own homes and families.

The church at Hook having so graciously supplied the accommodation was one thing, but setting up home on my own was another. I needed to rethink strategy for housekeeping, shopping and socializing. No servants here!

There were so many little things, such as what to do with empty tins when there were no children needing them for drinking purposes, what to do with vegetable peelings when there were no goats around to feed. A neighbour showed me what to do when she saw a pile of tins in the kitchen. There was no recycling in those days, and I felt guilty putting peelings into the garbage bags.

To investigate the supermarket the first time on my own scared me. There were so many brands of tea, coffee, mayonnaise, of everything; there was far too much from which to choose. I left the shop not knowing what to buy and not buying anything. One learns the hard way of course.

I was blessed with a caring and thoughtful church fellowship, and several took me under their wing and guided me through the intricacies of Social Services, bus passes, which shops to use and where to find them, which doctor and dentist to visit, etc. So many came and patiently explained things, such as the bills which would come and when and how to budget for them, which was very needful, for I had hardly any capital.

It was marvellous to go to bed at night and know I would not be called out to deal with emergencies. Cooking was a problem, as I was not used to it, though housework presented no problems. Learning to cook, I made many mistakes and had to eat them: missionaries never waste food. Gardening was another problem. I had to ask one of my brothers to identify some of the plants and what I needed to do for them. Even after all these years I am still learning, and it is not my favourite occupation.

God has given me a very special family in Hook Evangelical Church. Some family members are more special than others, which is inevitable in a large fellowship, but one problem remains. In Africa, as in other mission countries, friendships are held loosely before God. Holidays, furloughs, or changes of location often meant a friend would never be seen again. Furloughs might be in another country, for not everyone came from one's home country. On the other hand, someone might go home, and before he or she returned, I would go home, and frequently that was that. So we learned to give our friends back to God and accept the status quo without grieving.

Now at home, folk have their own special circle of friends more or less permanently, and though one is welcomed, it is always with the feeling of being an outsider. The circle closed when we first went away and carried on quite happily without us, but coming home to pick up the threads is different. As one friend explained it, we function on a different plane now; our priorities have changed. This is not a complaint, but I am trying to explain it as it affects the missionary on retirement.

WONDERFUL PROVIDENCES

Did being at home now mean that I no longer had need of special help from God? Far from it! How else could I explain the fact that I found a job almost on the doorstep, so to speak, doing part-time nursing, work I love, in a high dependency unit? On my first day there, I wondered how best to witness that I was a committed Christian—but God had it all in hand.

While helping a young male care assistant make a bed, I asked him whether he was a student working the long vacation. It happened to be his last day there that week. Before, he had been a seminary student for the Roman Catholic priesthood, but realized it was not his calling and left before it was too late. He then asked me what I did prior to going there. The conversation went like this:

'I was a missionary in Africa,' I said. The young man then said, 'I've just read a book called *Missing, believed killed* written by a missionary in Africa. In fact, I've read it three times! The name of the author is Margaret Hayes. Have you by any chance met her?' At this I laughed and said, 'I know the book. In fact, I wrote it.' At this he looked at me with incredulity, saw my name badge, and almost lost control of his hands, as sheets and blankets got all mixed up. He then ran off and told everybody who would listen who I was and what I had written. So within a couple of hours all the staff and most of the patients knew I was a Christian.

I needed a car, but did not have the wherewithal to purchase one, so how did I get one? Again, God engineered circumstances. A year after my return to England I went back to Niger to relieve Heather Barrow for her furlough. In total I was away for seven months, and God so overruled that my pension was not paid into my account. When eventually I returned home I collected the accrued amount, and it was the exact amount I needed to buy a second-hand car and pay the insurance on it at the same time. Once again, God showed himself to me in a fantastic and wonderful way.

One day I returned home after a period of gale force winds, and noticed that a large section of fencing had been blown down on to a bed of daffodils which were almost in bud. I decided to go out and move the fence but, just at that precise moment, Henry my cat came to me and told me he was hungry.

I spent the next five minutes organizing his food and, as I did so, I heard a very loud crash outside the kitchen window. A large chunk of the corner of the roof had landed right in the middle of the fence I was going to move! Well, 'Thank you, Lord,' was all I could keep saying for the next five minutes and, 'Thank you for Henry too!'

In 1991 I obtained three months leave of absence and went back to Galmi to relieve a missionary for a short furlough. God in a miraculous way met that financial need too. Right up to the evening before I left, I still needed £200 more to cover expenses. I had told no one but the Lord that I was still short of funds, but in answer to my prayers, the full amount was given to me on that last evening. It is exciting to be God's child.

Now as I write in this new century, there is change in nearly every area of life, but God is unchangeable, always the same, always there when needed most, and always present when we are frequently—alas!—unaware of him.

Someone gave me a copy of this poem, and I would like to leave it with you, my reader.

I'LL NEVER KNOW

I'll never know this side of heaven
What prayer poured forth has wrought,
In family, friends, and those I do not know
And yet for whom I pray.
I'll never know this side of heaven
What methods God will use to answer prayer.
Nor will I know how many times another's prayer
Has put my hand into the Father's when faced with need.
I'll never know this side of heaven
How many times my God has eased discouragements
Or sickness, pain or danger, grief or fear
Through power unleashed by kneeling saints.
I'll never know 'till I reach heaven
Why God fulfils His purposes through feeble praying saints.
But this I know, that when I pray
My lips present to God man's highest service
Reaching round the world with cosmic speed.

For prayer He tells me moves Omnipotence ...
Ask in My name and I will do it!

Written by Leona Mason, SIM missionary in Ghana

Nurse—prisoner of the rebel army

The villagers crowded round as I waited for the rebels to come. They were not particularly hostile but neither were they friendly. I noticed that one man was wearing a pair of my shoes; and it suddenly occurred to me that the last time I had seen them was in my bedroom a month before. He saw me looking at them and said, 'They were in your house and fit me nicely. We have taken all your things away.' I asked what my crime was. He answered by pointing first to his own skin and then to mine. 'You are white and a friend of the American capitalists,' he said.

After a short while of this intense scrutiny, a car arrived and two rebel officers got out. They had come to collect me, and pushed me rudely into the car. The journey was very short, and did not really necessitate the use of a car, but the rebels did not want to get wet in the rain as this would result in the loss of the power of magic on their bodies. I was already soaking wet so it didn't matter to me.

I recognized the car as having belonged to the doctor who had been at Banalia. It still had a few family belongings inside it, including his daughter's chemistry notebook from school. For some reason, the sight of this book comforted me. I wondered if the doctor had been rescued during the liberation of Stanleyville.

When we arrived at the house they had commandeered as their base, I was pushed into a large room while somebody was despatched to call the senior major. I could see out to the verandah, which was full of dancing women, chanting all the time. Many of them were former patients of mine at Bopepe, but although they must have recognized me, they did not acknowledge my presence in any way.

There are many better ways of celebrating Christmas Eve than being in a room full of Simbas armed with rifles, spears and knives. Those with spears and knives were dancing round me, brandishing their spears and thrusting them almost into my face. Their dancing was very insinuating and revolting, though I dared not show my feelings. One Simba, who was particularly repulsive in his actions, came to me and said he was going to have the greatest pleasure in thrusting his spear through my face. I almost believed him. Another approached me with a long, thin hunting knife and said he had been delegated to cut my throat that afternoon.

How do you pray in that kind of situation? I just called, 'Help!' Almost immediately my fear left me, and I raised my head to see just how ridiculous the whole situation was—these big brave men dancing round me as though I was a prize elephant they had just killed.

'You are a Protestant missionary, aren't you? Well then, you will not mind dying, as you believe you will go to heaven.' I answered in the affirmative, and added that I hoped he had the same assurance. He then asked if I was afraid to die, and when I said I was not, he looked at me for a long time then slowly said he really believed me.

This ludicrous situation probably only lasted some fifteen minutes, but it seemed like an hour. Eventually we heard someone shouting orders, the door behind me was opened and the short stocky figure of the major entered, followed by his retinue. I must have looked a sorry sight, my hair wet, uncombed for four days and hanging round my ears, my dress dirty, wet and torn, my legs swollen from infection, and sandals only half on my feet.

His immediate reaction was to order a chair for me, and when I was seated, he turned to interrogate me. He was just over five feet tall, in other words the same height as me, middle-aged, clean-shaven and with a kindly face. He wore a leopardskin sleeveless jacket and khaki shorts. Round his neck, together with numerous medicine charms, was a human thumb.

'Are you the white woman from Bopepe? Where have you been? How did you get here?' I answered that I was indeed the white woman, and that I had given myself up in order to prevent further bloodshed. I added, 'If you want to kill me, go ahead, but please leave my friends alone.' To my surprise he said, 'You are not going to die; we want you to work.' He then turned on his heels and walked out leaving me quite deflated and wondering just what lay ahead. I could only pray silently, asking for grace to meet this next phase of my life.

One of his officers, a lieutenant, stayed behind and ordered the Simbas to leave me alone. He also arranged for some food for me. Lieutenant Dieu Donné was very friendly, even sympathetic. He drew a chair up to a table, and motioned for me to sit across from him. He began to interrogate me about my life both before and after coming to Congo. He told me that he was a Catholic, but had spent four years in the UFM primary school at our station at Ekoko, and subsequently had been a bank clerk in Stanleyville. Everything I said was taken down to be used in their statement for or against me.

Half way through all this, the door reopened and a woman was brought in. The lieutenant asked me if I knew her. I certainly did. This was Mama Ruta, as we all called her, my faithful helper in the maternity unit and the wife of Bo's brother who had helped to release the wounded Simba.

When they were satisfied that we really did know each other, she was taken out again with her guard. I was disturbed at seeing Mama Ruta under such conditions, and asked why she was there. I was told they were holding her on two counts, primarily as a hostage until I gave myself up, and secondarily, because the villagers had taken a rifle from the wounded Simba. Until this was returned, she would remain a prisoner.

A little later a plate of pineapple was brought in for me, and proceedings stopped while I ate it. I must have been ravenous as the officer remarked on how hungry I was. Perhaps my table manners momentarily deserted me! The interrogation continued for a while, but stopped again when a plate of rice and mushrooms appeared, complete with a spoon to eat with. They also brought a mug of water.

When the interrogation was finally over, I was sent to the part of the village which had been turned into a prison. Mama Ruta had been told to prepare hot water for me to wash in, and they even gave me some soap. I was grateful for this, though I wished I had a towel. I put my dirty clothes on again, then combed my hair with a comb someone lent me. I now felt better able to face my captors. My legs and feet were the cause of much concern and a 'nurse' was sent to treat them.

I sat with Mama Ruta. Her 'prison' was a filthy hovel where she had to sleep on boards. We did not speak to each other at first, as many people were standing round us, but when we were finally left alone we started to talk. She was almost sick with worry, for they kept telling her that her husband was dead. She also asked me where Bo had hidden the rifle. She was very surprised when I told her that it was actually her husband who had hidden it, but if he was dead, how would anyone find it?

We discussed the fact that this was Christmas Eve, and were able to laugh at the incongruity of our situation. I dare not let my thoughts dwell too much on what was happening at home, such as carols, presents, parties and all the other Christmas celebrations. Were my parents mourning me? I expected they were, and in such circumstances would probably have cancelled any festivities that year.

I had hoped to be back home for Christmas, but for some reason God saw fit to allow me to share in the meanness and poverty of that first Christmas long ago, when Christ, the Babe of Bethlehem was born in a stable. I looked around me. Chickens were scratching everywhere, half-starved dogs moped about in the dirt, and the raucous voices of men who had been drinking grated on our ears. Was it possible that Joseph had led Mary to the stable in similar conditions when Bethlehem was overcrowded, and there was no room in the inn? Christmas cards depict the stable as being clean and wholesome, but I doubt if it really was.

'In everything give thanks'—I felt rebuked as I reflected on that verse, yet I was able to thank the Lord for sending his Son into the world in order that the world might be saved, and for allowing me the privilege of sharing in some of his sufferings.

More food was brought which Mama Ruta had prepared—rice and peanut butter. She did not eat any herself, in fact I was told she had not touched any food for days. I was very hungry and ate heartily.

The rain cleared, and the women I had seen when I first arrived began to dance in the open. They were fairly near to us, and Mama Ruta thought it would be a good idea for me to try and speak to them. So I hobbled over, and as I approached, I recognized the young wife of one of our evangelists. She saw me looking at her, and turned her head away. Absolutely no one would acknowledge me, so I sadly made my way back to Mama Ruta, who could sense how upset I was, and just sat holding my hand.

It was 5pm before the Simbas let the women go back to their villages, and then it was that one woman, who was 'president of the political group' in her village, who came and asked me to go and see them. As I approached this time, the group suddenly broke up and they all came running towards me and hugged me. Many wept openly at my plight, and they were all concerned at how thin I was. I really valued their friendship in a world which had suddenly become so hostile. This show of affection made a lovely Christmas present especially after being ignored a few minutes earlier. I do not think they had ever been really against me. It was simply that they were very afraid of the Simbas, and had felt too vulnerable even to acknowledge me.

Shortly after this, the major came back. I could hear him calling first to one and then another of the officers to go to him. I was given some more food before being ordered to present myself to him. Mama Ruta took my hand and whispered that she would pray for me.

I was treated more kindly this time, being ushered—as opposed to being pushed—into a small bedroom in a mud-walled house. It was dark, with only two makeshift palm-oil lamps for light. The major was sitting on the edge of the bed in his underpants! By his side was his wife of the moment, a young arrogant girl. On the floor in front of them was their supper of rice and fish. They ate with their fingers and spat the bones on the floor in time-honoured fashion.

A chair was brought for me and I was ordered to sit down facing them. So I sat and watched them eat. The major then interviewed several other people and listened to their complaints before bellowing for Lieutenant Dieu Donné to come in with his report about me. I was asked leading questions and every time I tried to answer the major would yell 'Liar!' until finally I said it was not much point me telling him anything as he did not believe me, so I would not say any more. At this he looked quite astounded and quietened down considerably. Was Mama Ruta praying? I'm sure she was. He asked if I knew where Bo had gone, and told me they had killed eight men at Bopepe. I felt sick with grief and guilt when I heard this, all the more so as he didn't seem to know who they were. Later a friendly Simba said only two had been killed, but even that was two too many.

His wife then locked the door from the inside. I began to feel very apprehensive. The major pointed to the bed, which was a wide king-size one, and said very gently, 'Do not be afraid, I will not touch you. Go right over to the other side of the bed, and my wife will sleep in the middle. Do not be afraid, I will protect you.' His wife then gave me a pillow which had come from Mary's bed, and one of her sheets too. I clambered over as best I could, as my legs were very painful and swollen, and after wrapping myself in Mary's sheet, lay down.

I prayed for protection for the night and grace to go through whatever was ahead of me. I also took time to thank the Lord for a roof over my head and a bed to sleep in. I fell asleep as soon as I had finished praying and slept soundly all night. When I awoke at 7.30am, I was alone in the room and judging by the noise outside, the day's activities had been under way for some time. Congolese are habitually early risers. How was I able to tell the time, as my watch had been confiscated at Banalia? Simply by observing the position of the sun, which on the equator is very predictable.

I opened a tiny window, and noticed in the daylight a number of details that I had not seen the previous evening. At the foot of the bed I saw the basket I had used for premature babies which used to be kept in my bedroom at Bopepe, and what was more it was filled with my clothes! There were some more hanging on a nail on the wall. The large mirror from our bathroom was resting on a chair by the bed, our cushions were being used for pillows, and the blanket used by the major had belonged to Mary.

As I tried to take all this in, the major's wife came in to tell me I was wanted outside. There was no need to dress, as I hadn't undressed. I could barely walk, as the infection had caused my feet to swell up so much that I could not wear my sandals. The major was genuinely sorry for me, and ordered the 'nurse' to treat me immediately.

Mama Ruta greeted me. She said that the rifle had been found and given back to the Simbas, so she was now technically free, but had been ordered to stay and look after the Mademoiselle. I was horrified at this and begged them to let her go. At about 4pm they finally consented, and she left me, very relieved to be going as by then most of the men were very drunk.

This was Christmas Day 1964, and while everyone in England was singing 'Peace on earth and goodwill toward men', I was sitting in the middle of a group of bloodthirsty Simbas. The Lord gave me peace in this situation, and even provided some good will in the shape of Lieutenant Dieu Donné, who brought out an accordion and asked me to name some carols. He then played 'Silent night', 'The first Noel' and 'Hark the herald angels sing' over and over again for an hour and a half. Our primary school at Ekoko had clearly done him some good, for although he had been to Yugoslavia and Moscow for military training, and subsequently told me that religion was the opiate of the people, he played carols on Christmas Day to comfort the heart of a lonely Protestant missionary and a prisoner at that.

My Christmas dinner was not turkey and roast potatoes but elephant meat and boiled rice. They gave me enormous helpings and were upset when I found it too much to manage, but it was not only the huge portions that caused me to struggle—elephant meat is very tough and requires a lot of chewing.

Lieutenant Dieu Donné asked if I had hidden a case or anything with some clothes somewhere in the jungle, for by this time my dress was torn, grubby and very much the worse for wear. Bo had told me where he had hidden my suitcase, but I wondered if I could remember the way. Nor was I at all keen to take any rebels anywhere near Bopepe again. However, Dieu Donné promised that he would take me to find it, and would be my personal bodyguard for the trip, but not on Christmas Day. If my legs and feet were better we would go the following Monday.

Several women from various villages turned up, along with some of the village elders who had been my patients at Bopepe. It was good to see them and exchange greetings, but they were very guarded in their conversations with me. One man started to say something about Paul Ponea, but another man near him immediately put a hand over his mouth. He knew the Simbas wanted me to believe that Paul was dead.

Many of the women were wearing my clothes—often after making some alterations to them. My uniforms had been cut in half to make blouses and underskirts, and one woman appeared wearing the top part of one of my nylon nightdresses. I didn't make any comments. Whether I was meant to notice I am not sure, but I thought silence would be the wisest policy. It was not so easy to remain silent when three days later the major appeared wearing a pair of shorts made out of some material I had used to make things for the nursery. It came in two colour schemes: little pale blue puppies with yellow bows on a pink background or pink puppies, again with yellow bows, on a blue background. On this occasion he wore pink with blue puppies. He must have found a tailor to make them, and was so proud of this splendid new garment he even took roll call in it. The other officers were jealous, so he had to give them some of the material, and they too visited the tailor. So this was the new uniform for the rebel army! Some wore pink, some blue, while others were dressed in patchwork made from odds and ends. I dared not laugh out loud, but inside I was almost hysterical.

Another officer carried his spare bullets in one of our bright green cushion-covers. He took it everywhere with him. It was good that there was no fighting at that time, as he would have had a hard time reloading his rifle in a hurry.

One young Simba, who could not have been more than seventeen, turned up one day wearing three of my pink and blue hair-curlers on his wrist, and the polythene tubing and glass connection of a blood-transfusion set round his neck. As if this was not enough, he had fixed two of our bright orange nylon pot-scourers to his cowboy-style hat and was wearing a pair of surgical gloves on his hands and a very worn out pair of wellington boots on his feet. He actually went on parade dressed like this, but nobody took any notice of him, except me, of course.

Another day the major turned up in Ruby Gray's full-length pale blue candlewick housecoat. The other men were very envious! Later that same day, he came out in Mary Baker's pink bathrobe, wearing it back to front until someone pointed out to him the buttons should be down the front.

Although these incidents were very amusing, the Simbas were very serious. It also underlines the huge cultural differences between us in the west and these men who were largely uneducated and had never travelled out of their own country.

On yet another occasion, the major's wife came to me wearing one of my own dresses and asked me if I would alter it to fit her. As I am small and slim and she was tall and buxom, it would have been impossible. However, it was not the logistics that made me refuse, it just seemed like the last straw when I was still wearing my filthy ragged dress. It would have been a better witness if I had at least made an attempt at altering it. This was brought home to me shortly afterwards when God brought Hebrews 10:34 into my mind. In this verse, the writer commended his readers for taking 'joyfully the spoiling of your goods, knowing in yourselves that ye have in heaven a better and an enduring substance.' I felt very convicted as I reflected on this verse, and asked God to forgive me for letting him down. Unfortunately, by this time, the woman had gone elsewhere with the dress so the opportunity to make amends was gone.

This incident, minor as it was, really brought home to me how much we like to hold on to our personal possessions. The Lord was going to teach me even more about taking the spoiling of my goods joyfully. It was painful, but I found that he gives grace even in the hardest of situations.

I had lost contact with the outside world; I had lost all my local friends, and now I was shortly to see our house and the little hospital I had founded in ruins. All ties were being severed one by one. I was beginning to learn what it was to be completely dependent on the Lord.

When Monday came, the swelling of my legs and feet had gone down to the point where I could put my sandals on again, so it was agreed that I should go with Lieutenant Dieu Donné and four other armed Simbas to find my suitcase.

On the way we ran into a group of Simbas who were very obnoxious to me, and it took all Dieu Donné's time to keep them under control. We passed another group, and I noticed that several of them were wearing our house aprons, one had my bath towel round his neck, and another carried a blanket of Mary's in a bucket. Dieu Donné said that if anything belonged to me I could take it if I wanted. I took the blanket and the towel. The Simbas were furious and called down curses on me, but I was elated at such a find.

As we neared Bopepe, we had to pass several other villages, and the one immediately before Bopepe had been totally gutted by fire; not a single house was left standing. Dieu Donné said it had been done because I had not given myself up. We finally arrived at Bopepe. It was deserted, which was no surprise considering every house had been burnt to the ground except the three with permanent roofs, Bo's, Asani's, and ours. The church, which was built of brick, was also comparatively intact.

We entered our house. A lot of the things in it had been given to us by friends, so they had a sentimental attachment besides any considerations of monetary value or usefulness. I am sure that a missionary's home almost always seems to be a place of peace and happiness because even the furniture and furnishings emanate the love of the givers, but there was no peace or happiness now. Everything that was portable had been taken, and large things that were too heavy to carry like the refrigerator, stove, dining-room table, and the treadle sewing-machine had been vandalized by machetes. I was horrified at the wanton destruction. Food which had been in tins or containers had been poured out on the floor. As the Simbas could not read any of the books in English, they had torn most of them up and strewn the pages over the floor. I found a Bible more or less intact, along with a few other books, including several medical textbooks, and these were put on one side to go back with us. How they escaped the vandalism I do not know, but I was especially pleased to find the Bible.

Next, we entered the forest and retrieved the suitcase. I am sure there were eyes watching us all the way in. The camp bed, water filter and Primus stove were in the same spot as my case and the Simbas wanted to take them too, but I asked Dieu Donné to leave them for the villagers, as they had lost so much because of me. He agreed, and ordered the Simbas only to take my suitcase, although I expect they came back later and helped themselves to the other things. I was hoping that maybe Bo would be able to get there first, as he could certainly find a use for them.

We returned to the village, and I had time to look round. I felt as though my heart was weeping, as I had such a pain in my chest. The village always used to be full of life, but now it was deserted, every house a ruin. I wondered where the owners had gone. I thought of George my nurse and his five small children, of Mikaele who had four little ones, the last having been one of my premature babies, of Alumba, Bwanachui and their respective families. Where were the village elders, those saintly, hard working and brave men? I wanted to cry as it hurt so much. Dieu Donné stood behind me and said very quietly, 'It was all your fault for hiding in the forest.' If he wanted to make me feel guilty, he succeeded. I asked, more in anger than anything else, but also with some curiosity, 'And what has this profited you, or the People's Army? Do you really think that such unnecessary destruction of innocent people's homes is going to endear the population to your cause?' He had no answer.

I opened the case when we got back to find that the ubiquitous white ants had found their way in, but only just, so we were able to clear them all away. The major's wife was with me as I tipped everything out for inspection, and if I had not been quick enough I am sure she would have taken all those clothes too. She did help herself to a cardigan when I was away one day, but that was all.

That evening I washed and dried myself like a civilized person and was finally able to put on clean clothes. When I emerged neat and tidy for the first time since giving myself up, they all applauded. I was rather touched by this; maybe even the Simbas weren't all bad, or was it simply that they were ashamed of my dirt and rags?

Now that I was clean and properly dressed, I was told it was time to begin work. I was to go to the hospital at Banalia, twelve miles away, and was to take or appropriate anything I thought would be necessary for dispensary work.

After my walk to Bopepe, my feet were very swollen again and the sores on my legs had not yet healed. The major didn't ask if I knew how to ride a bicycle, but ordered his men to find me one, so I could ride to Banalia. How did they find a bicycle? They simply stopped the first cyclist who had a lady's bicycle and appropriated it. It was almost brand new, and I felt quite sorry for the owner, who would have needed to save for months to buy it, unless, of course, it had been stolen.

We set out for Banalia at 6am next morning. The major had told me I would need a sponge bag and a blanket, as we would be staying overnight. As I was still sleeping in my clothes, I didn't need a nightdress. Two things were missing from my sponge bag; a comb and toothpaste. The major had taken them, so I simply took them back. When I told him afterwards, he just laughed.

About thirty Simbas were going to Banalia, including the major. On this occasion he was wearing a long button-through beige dress, with large red buttons, which reached to his feet. He walked all the way to Banalia in it.

It was wonderful to be able to cycle ahead of the crowd and I was pleased that the major trusted me to go alone. It gave me the chance to pray without being disturbed. It was hardly true freedom, but I made the most of it.

An incident occurred on the way which shows just how brutal even the youngest Simbas could be. A coloured boy of twelve years and another boy of eleven had been included in the group going to Banalia. They were my official bodyguards. The coloured boy had been brought up with his white father and Congolese mother, but when the troubles began, his father went back to his own country, leaving the boy with his mother, so he promptly joined the rebel army. A handsome boy, better educated and somewhat more cultured than most of the others, he was usually polite to me, though occasionally very cynical.

At one point of the journey, which he was also making by bicycle, he was quite a way in front of me and pulled up at a village to wait. The few villagers who were left promptly fled into the jungle, apart from an elderly blind man and his wife. The boy saw them going, and called them to come back, but they took no notice and continued to run.

The boy, who was called 'Panya' (the Rat) by the other Simbas, remounted his bicycle and returned to the rest of the group to tell them about this.

By this time I had reached the village and was talking to the blind man. He was very bewildered and when I told him I was white, he became very frightened and wanted to hide with the others. At this point, the Rat came back with several officers and the other young boy. They were very angry and grabbed the old man, ordering him to show them the way to the forest. Only when I pointed out the obvious fact that he was blind did they eventually leave him alone.

The Rat then decided to look for himself and came back with a young woman who was in an advanced stage of pregnancy. To my utter horror and disgust, he kicked her in the abdomen, then hit her over the head with his rifle-butt as she bent over, while screaming at her to tell him where her husband was hiding. One of the officers—a grown man—then took over and hit her several times in the back with his rifle-butt until she was on the point of collapsing. When she had recovered sufficiently, she took them into the jungle and about five minutes later they flushed out an elderly man who emerged holding a machete. They then jumped on him, knocking him down and hitting him with their rifle-butts. The old blind man was absolutely terrified by all this, so I led him into the house where I assumed he lived. The rest of the group of Simbas arrived at this point and promptly started vandalizing the village, breaking every window and door they could find.

I watched helplessly, feeling physically sick. The only crime the elderly man had committed was to be afraid of the Simbas and take to his heels when he saw them coming. As a punishment, he was forced to go to Banalia—at the run, and accompanied by my two 'bodyguards'. As he ran, the Rat would cycle behind him, deliberately causing his front wheel to run into the man's legs, which made him stumble, at which point the other boy would threaten him with a long knife. We were approximately five miles from Banalia, and he was made to run all the way under those conditions at the hottest time of the day. The pregnant woman was also taken prisoner on the same charge of being afraid, but she was allowed to walk.

There was an appalling lack of logic about the rebels. They terrorized everyone by their brutality, but seemed surprised that this made people afraid of them. What also saddened me was how young the Rat and his child accomplice were, yet they had already been trained to hate.